Faith From

A MOTHER'S SOUL MOVES MOUNTAINS

MARY ALBERT

INSPIRED BY RENEE WILLIAMS

ISBN: 979-8-89031-589-2 (sc)
ISBN: 979-8-89031-590-8 (hc)
ISBN: 979-8-89031-591-5 (e)

Because of the dynamic nature of the Internet, any web addresses or links contained in this book may have changed since publication and may no longer be valid. The views expressed in this work are solely those of the author and do not necessarily reflect the views of the publisher, and the publisher hereby disclaims any responsibility for them.

THE EWINGS
PUBLISHING

One Galleria Blvd., Suite 1900, Metairie, LA 70001
(504) 702-6708
1-888-421-2397

DEDICATION

We dedicate *Faith From – A Mother's Soul Moves Mountains* to our Lord and Savior, Jesus Christ. Without Him, none of this would have been possible.

Mary Albert & Renee Williams

CONTENTS

Acknowledgements vii
Prologue ix

Chapter 1   Anticipation 1
Chapter 2   Pulling the Team Together 11
Chapter 3   Expectation. 25
Chapter 4   Milestones. 43
Chapter 5   New Beginnings 49
Chapter 6   Unexpected Blessings 57
Chapter 7   From Out of Nowhere. 63
Chapter 8   On a Mission 71
Chapter 9   What Next?. 77
Chapter 10 And the Drama Begins 87
Chapter 11 Stand on His Word 97
Chapter 12 A New Day is Dawning 107

Epilogue 115
Meet the Inspiration 117
Meet the Author 119

ACKNOWLEDGEMENTS

I would like to acknowledge and thank everyone that has helped me with this book:

To my Lord and Savior Jesus Christ who put the dream seed inside of me to write and helped me connect with all the wonderful people on this page.

To my Mom and Dad who always told me 'the world is your oyster' you can do and be whatever you want to be.

To my brother Frank, for his encouragement and support through the process.

To Dr. Michael Chitwood, for without him this book would have never been. For it was at his conference that I met and became friends with the inspiration for this book Ms. Renee Williams. Thank you, Dr. Chitwood for always encouraging me to follow my dreams and to never give up on them.

To Renee Williams for being my friend and letting me be part of sharing her Faith Story with the World.

With much love and many blessings, I thank you all.

Mary, July 2019.

I would also want to acknowledge my family, friends and all my church family: Lodebar Church and Ministries Bethsaida MB Church, Tabernacle Baptist Church, Abundant Life Teaching Center, Victory Apostolic Church of God and ICCM.

Renee July 2019

PROLOGUE

*'For I consider that the sufferings of this present time
are not worthy to be compared with the glory which
shall be revealed in us.'*

Romans 8:18

Karen believed in marriage and having both parents
there to raise the children. But when one's spouse
says they don't want to be married any more what
choice does one have but to divorce. After four years
of marriage and two years of separation Karen finds
herself a divorced devoted mother of four-year old
twins working as a supervisor at a financial institution
in Minneapolis to make ends meet. She put her trust
and faith in God and knew He would be their provider.

Karen had learned about the Lord in her early
twenties when her faith journey began, but It was after
her divorce that she felt her faith start growing. Life
just seemed to go along with a few bumps in the road
here and there.

She soon found that just because one has faith in Jesus, the way is not always smooth. Her faith is rocked and tested when her son David goes from having what was thought to be just a bad cold to fighting for his life in less than two weeks after Christmas break.

A mother's love crosses all boundaries and for her child the most intense feeling; knowing that God holds David's life in his hands as well as her heart. Karen knew there was no room for negativity or negative people as she embarked on the toughest part of her faith journey. Focusing on the Lord Jesus Christ and his promise to her for her children David and Denise.

Praise, pray and stand on His word was all Karen could do. For she knew she had to trust her *Faith from* Him, the Almighty One.

Chapter 1

ANTICIPATION

*'Commit your works to the Lord, and your thoughts
will be established.'*

Proverbs 16:3

inding a home in the suburbs was top priority
on Karen's list for the year, as she did not want
her twins attending an inner-city high school. Like
many single mothers, Karen wanted the best for her
children and to give them every advantage in life that
she could. Despite the upheaval, she was prepared to
make the necessary sacrifices and to move her family
into a good school district for her twins to receive the
best education she could find.

Through all the ups and downs of life, and in
trying to keep a steady and stable homelife for her
children, Karen relied on the cornerstone of faith. For

1

this move to happen, Karen knew in her heart that she needed the Lord more than ever. Karen's modus operandi throughout life was to offer every decision, no matter how big or small, over to the Lord in prayer. She knew that what she was asking for was a big ask with her limited budget, but she trusted in God that the move out to Plymouth from the inner-city would be a small thing for Him. Such was her faith in placing God in the middle of her decision, that she knew He would make a way for it all to happen and for it all to come together under His guidance and divine plan. He had never let her down. He was the Way Maker. Through Him, she had always been able to provide for those she was blessed to call her own.

For Karen, the plan to move her family to a new home was revealed to her during a devotional reading of the prophet Jeremiah.

> 'For I know the thoughts that I think toward you," says the LORD, "thoughts of peace not of evil, to give a future and a hope.' Jer. 29:11

The moment she accepted this revelation in her heart, Karen handed it all over to the Lord and prayed:

> 'Thank you, Lord. I believe that You have and will continue to make me prosper. You have always provided for my family's needs. You are the wonderful Jehovah-Jireh. Lord, my hope for the future is to give David and Denise the best start for their adult life that I can. I want them to have the very best education that will form them over the coming years.

I don't know how all this will happen, but I know that You will continue to provide and give me the guidance as to what I should do. I ask this in Your mighty name. Amen.'

From that moment, Karen felt the plan coming together. She knew that her first step was to sell the family home. Without fear nor doubt, Karen immediately phoned the realtor who had sold her the house she and her family were currently living in. As the phone rang, Karen thought back fondly to the time when she was pregnant with the twins, and how this home had been a prayer answered all those years ago.

The phone was answered.

'Hello, Sunshine Reality,' spoke the familiar voice, 'Daisy speaking.'

'Hello Daisy, you are just the person I was hoping to speak with,' Karen replied, as a smile crept across her face. 'This is Karen Bonner. I don't know if you'll remember me, but fourteen years ago you sold me my first home. I was pregnant with twins at the time.'

That was all Karen had to say for the connection to be made.

'Of course, I remember you!' Daisy exclaimed. 'I had to find you the perfect home to bring those precious babies' home to. So, how are those young ones? If I remember correctly you had a boy and a girl.'

'Yes, I did. Can you believe they'll be starting high school in the fall?'

With an easy rhythm of two old friends catching up, they spoke for several minutes about the twins and how life had been good to them in the home Daisy had found for them all those years ago.

'I take it from the conversation that you're looking to sell and move up?' Daisy eventually asked, sensing that this was the purpose behind Karen's call.

'I guess I am,' Karen laughed. 'With the twins starting high school in the fall, I want them to be living closer to a better school. Daisy, I want you to find us the perfect home out in the Plymouth area so we can be in the Wayzata school district.'

'I'd be delighted to work with you again,' Daisy said. 'Let me get to work finding some options for you and I'll swing by your house tomorrow so we can discuss what needs to be done to get it ready for the market. What time would be best for you?'

'Would an evening appointment around six work?'

'Six o'clock is perfect,' Daisy replied. 'I look forward to seeing you then.'

Hanging up the phone, Karen felt a great peace come over her, and she knew that this was the right thing to do. Lifting her eyes to heaven, Karen smiled and thanked the Lord.

Daisy wasted no time in getting the search underway. As planned, she arrived at Karen's home the following evening. When she drove up to the front door, she remembered showing the house to the then pregnant Karen. Not all her clients she remembered, but Karen she did for she was such a sweet young woman on the verge of motherhood. She even remembered dropping by the family home after the twins were born, as she could not resist seeing the babies, to bring them a little 'welcome home' basket. Lost in her thoughts, Daisy turned to look as Karen opened the door, and in that moment, she felt a great contentment when she saw the familiar bright smile of Karen Bonner.

'Come in,' Karen invited, as she led the way into the living room. 'Make yourself comfortable, Daisy. May I get you something to drink?'

'I'm fine dear,' Daisy said, as she looked around. 'I love how you've decorated. Before we sit and talk, would you mind giving me a quick tour of the house?'

'Sure,' Karen replied, before leading the way.

As they toured the house, they finally came to the kitchen where the twins were doing their homework.

'These must be the twins,' Daisy cried. 'My, how they have grown.'

Karen introduced Denise and David and told them that Daisy was one of their first visitors when they came home from the hospital.

'It's nice to meet you,' David said, 'but I have to tell you that I don't really remember you.'

Daisy laughed before replying. 'But I remember you… and that smile of yours is just like your Momma's.'

Leaving the twins to complete their homework, Karen and Daisy finished their tour before heading back to the living room to sit down and talk.

'What do you think?' Karen asked.

'You've done a great job with the house,' Daisy replied, as she took a black property portfolio from her bag. 'However, there are a few things you'll need to do to get it ready before we put the house on the market.'

As they talked, Daisy made a short list of what Karen needed to do.

'I'm impressed with the work you've had done on the place and how great your home looks,' Daisy said, handing her list over to Karen. 'For us to sell the most important thing you must do on this list is declutter. Buyers need to feel they are walking into their future home, not someone else's.'

Karen smiled, for she knew Daisy was right.

After going through the rest of the list, they chatted a bit longer before Karen walked Daisy to the door.

'I'll be in touch,' Daisy said.

'Thanks for coming over.'

'My pleasure.'

After closing the door and leaning against it, Karen felt so happy, almost giddy inside, excited that she was starting out on a new adventure. Looking down at the list in her hand, the good news for her was that the 'to-do' list, for putting the house on the market, was not too long. Daisy had only written three things on the list:

1. Declutter the entire house - Less is More.
2. Replace missing piece of trim at the front door.
3. Think about some fresh paint in the kitchen and bedrooms.

I can do this, Karen thought. *'Get the twins and Ivan onboard with this, and it can be done quickly.'*

Over the coming days, Daisy and Karen spoke more about a reasonable time frame for getting everything on the list completed. The target date to put out the

'For Sale' sign was set for May; soon after Karen had one final Mother's Day in the home where she had raised her babies.

When Karen finally put in a call to her brother Ivan, it went straight to voicemail. Typical of him not to answer the phone, she rolled her eyes as she waited for the automated recording to end before she left him a message.

'Hey, brother, haven't seen your ugly mug for a while. Why don't you come over and have dinner with us this week? I'll have your favorite, Egg Foo Young. Hit me back and let me know what night works for you. Love you, bye.'

She did not have to wait long before Ivan returned the call. Twenty minutes after leaving the message, Karen found herself reading Ivan's name on the caller-ID.

'Hi Ivan', she answered. 'I was wondering if you'd like to...'

He cut her off.

'Karen, Karen, Karen! Having me over for my favorite meal can only mean that something is up? So, spill it sis!'

'Can't a sister have her favorite Brother over for dinner cuz she misses him?' she humored.

'Since when? And for the record I'm your only brother. Plus, I'm ninety-nine percent sure that a call with an offer of dinner means you have something for me to do. So, what did you break?'

'Nothing!' she replied, wondering how to phrase the words to ask him. 'But... I do have a honey-do list that I need help with. Will you help me out?'

Ivan chuckled. 'I think I need to know what's on the list before I say yes.'

'Just come over for dinner and I'll tell you everything.'

'Guess I'll be seeing you tomorrow then,' Ivan replied. 'And the Egg Foo Young better be from Szechuan Spice.'

'I've got you covered,' Karen reassured him as she punched the air. 'See you tomorrow at seven.'

The moment she hung up the phone, Karen jumped into the air and squealed with sheer delight, causing her daughter Denise to come running out to her.

'Mom, what's up?'

'Nothing much, just made dinner plans with Uncle Ivan for tomorrow night.'

'Guess that means we're either having Egg Foo Young or Pizza'

'Don't be such a smarty pants, young lady.' Karen replied, trying to look strict before they both burst out laughing as David walked into the room.

'Spill it! What's so funny?'

'David Ivan Bonner, what is with the *spill it*? You are starting to sound just like your uncle Ivan.'

Once again, Karen couldn't keep a straight face, and such was her joy she once again burst out laughing.

'Uncle Ivan's coming for dinner tomorrow night.' Karen explained to David.

'Yes!' he cried out, as he started jigging around the room. 'We can play the new race game I just got.'

'I'm sure he'll play a round or two, but I get him first. I've some things that I need to discuss with him. After we're done, he's all yours.'

At the end of a long day, and after getting the twins to bed, Karen took a moment to acknowledge the happiness she was feeling. Kneeling beside her bed, she closed her eyes and began to pray:

'Lord Jesus, I just want to thank you for today. Thank You for breathing life into my dream for providing a better life for my children and for giving me the plan to make the move out to Plymouth. I thank you for lining up the people that I will need to make this happen. Bless Daisy so that she will find us the perfect house again. I thank you for my brother Ivan, for giving him a loving, caring and helpful spirit. Let him see the plan and be onboard with it. Lord, I need his help because I don't have the means to pay a laborer for the things that need to be done. Lord, if it's not Ivan, then please put someone in my path that can help me. You have blessed me with two wonderful children; help them to see the overall reasoning of the move. I want to give them the best I can, but I know moving to a new area and a new school will be difficult. Please help them be happy and think of it as a new adventure and not that I'm pulling them away from their friends. Finally, God my loving Father, I thank you for your son Jesus, the Way Maker who is making the way for all of us. I pray this in Your mighty name, Amen.'

That night, as she drifted into sleep, Karen felt a sense of calm come over her, knowing that everything would all work out according to plan - God's plan.

Chapter 2

PULLING THE TEAM TOGETHER

'For in fact the body is not one member but many.'

1 Corinthians 12:14

It was a hectic Friday and it went in quickly. At the end of her working day, Karen phoned in the dinner order to Szechuan Spice so she could pick it up on the way home. Then calling Ivan, she left him a message to let him know that she was leaving and that she had ordered him a double portion of Egg Foo Young.

On the way home she hit some major traffic, so decided to exit the freeway and use the side streets. It was only when she was exiting that she realize that it would probably take just as long driving through the backed up side streets as it would have if she had stayed on the freeway, but she had to keep moving even if it was at a snail's pace; it was still movement, unlike the freeway that was at a dead stop.

A little later than she had anticipated, she finally saw the restaurant up ahead and began looking for a parking spot. Noticing a young woman heading towards her car, Karen slowed down and stopped so the woman could back out and she could have the spot. Horns blasted behind her to keep moving, but she was not going to give up the parking spot. Turning on her hazard lights, she smiled before waving at the person in the car behind her who was now making a rude gesture with his right hand.

As the young woman reversed out of the parking spot, she waved at Karen and mouthed a thank you, knowing that by holding back the traffic Karen had made it easier for her to back out onto the congested main road. As soon as she was on her way Karen pulled in, thanking the Lord for giving her the spot.

Walking to the restaurant, Karen felt her phone buzz. It was a text from Ivan:

'Traffic is horrible but I'm on my way. Don't eat my Egg Foo Young.' The message ended with a smiley emoji.

Karen was shocked when she opened the door to the restaurant and saw the number of people inside.

Has half of Minneapolis decided to eat from Szechuan Spice tonight? she wondered.

The line was so long that it took twenty minutes to get up to the counter and pay for her takeout. Thankfully, they had been so busy that her order had just come up, so it would still be warm when she got it home.

Returning to her car, Karen worried that she would have trouble backing out onto the main road with all the traffic coming her way. Putting her car in reverse, her backup lights signaled her intent. Expecting to be there for some time, she was amazed to see a car stop and flash for her to reverse out; just like she had done with the young woman. The irony was not lost, and as she pulled out, she thanked the man in the car before turning and thanking the Lord.

The normal ten-minute drive from Szechuan Spice to her house took her twenty-five minutes. Turning onto her street, she saw Ivan on the front lawn tossing a football to David. It did her heart good to see them. Knowing there was a male figure in her children's lives, that did not have drama all wrapped up in a complicated relationship, was another reason why she relied on Ivan for his help.

As Karen pulled into the driveway and parked, Ivan and David came over to the car and waited for her to get out.

'David, can you get the food and my work bag from the passenger seat and take them inside please?' she asked as she opened the door, but Ivan ran around and opened the passenger door before David could.

'You took so long I just want to make sure my dinner is really in the bag.' Ivan said in jest, grinning at Karen before looking into the bag. 'Okay, looks like it's all there. Here you go David. No opening that bag until we all get inside.'

Taking the Chinese food bag from his uncle, David waited for his mom's work bag to be handed to him.

'Go on, I'll bring this in,' Ivan said, as he picked up Karen's work bag and threw the strap across his shoulder before closing the car door.

As he turned to walk towards the house, Karen had hurried around the car to block his path. She put her hand out to stop him.

'I want to talk to you briefly before we have dinner with the twins,' she said.

'What is it sis?' he asked, his eyes filled with concern as he scanned Karen's face.

'I need you to help me fix a few things around the house.'

'I kind of got that as you usually don't offer up dinner without a honey-do project that needs doing. Spill it.'

Karen turned and looked up at the area above the door where the trim was missing, pointed and said. 'Jobs like that.'

'I don't know how to do that!' Ivan replied, as he looked up to where the trim was missing.

'Seriously, Ivan? You know if I call someone to fix it, they'll tell me some story about having to remove all the siding just to get that piece of trim replaced. Please, help me so I'm not taken on by some contractor. You were so upset the last time I hired a laborer to do something, that you told me you could have done it for a lot less.'

Ivan looked at her, remembering he had told her to come to him first before calling any contractors to do work for her.

'Is that all?' Ivan asked.

'No,' Karen sighed. 'I need to paint the kitchen and the bedrooms too.'

'Do you know how much stuff is in the kids' bedrooms? That's going to be a super hard job unless you clean out the bedrooms so I can do them right.'

'We will do that for you.'

'How?' Ivan asked, not quite believing her.

Karen knew there was no time like the present to tell him of her plan.

'We're moving.'

'What? What are you talking about? When?'

'Not far away. Just to Plymouth to get the kids into a better school district for high school,' she explained, barely catching a breath.

'But that's the fall,' Ivan interrupted, as he reached out and touched her arm. 'That's less than six months away.'

'Um, not really,' Karen sheepishly replied. 'We only have about two months. The realtor and I have talked about it. To be ready for the optimum selling season, I need to put the for sale sign out the weekend after Mother's Day.'

'What?' Ivan exclaimed in a rather harsh tone, as he took a step back. 'You've already talked to a realtor?'

'Yes. Remember, Daisy the lady that sold us this house?'

Ivan nodded.

'Well, she came over and we talked. She looked around and gave me a list of three things I need to do before I put the house on the market.' Then, using her fingers to count them off, she continued. 'One the trim,' as she pointed back towards the front door. 'Two the painting. Three, we're going to need to declutter the whole house.'

The third one made Ivan laugh out loud.

'Sis, you're gonna need more than two months to get all that done. You all have so much...' then using his index and middle fingers on each hand he made quotation marks in the air... 'Clutter.' He made the air quotations again as he said, 'aka stuff. 'lots of stuff'

As they were talking, they were interrupted by Denise who opened the front door.

'Are you guys coming?' she asked, somewhat frustrated. 'We're hungry.'

'Did you set the table?' Karen asked, as she turned to face her daughter.

'Yes, I know what to do so we can eat,' Denise replied, before disappearing back into the house.

'Make sure to wash your hands. We are coming right now.' Karen shouted after her. Just as they were about to walk up the steps, she reached out and took Ivan's hand and squeezed it. 'Thank you, brother. I knew I could count on you.'

Ivan looked at her and smiled. 'I haven't said yes, yet.'

'We'll see,' Karen replied with a chuckle, as she followed him up the steps and into the house.

Taking off their coats, Karen hung them up in the hall closet while Ivan dropped her work bag in the living room by her small desk. Then entering a small downstairs bathroom, he went to wash his hands while Karen made her way to the kitchen.

'David why didn't you take the food out of the bag?' Karen asked, when she noticed the food sitting in the middle of the table still in the bag.

'Not until Uncle Ivan comes in here so he knows that no one's been in his dinner.'

As David was speaking, Ivan walked in and grabbed him, giving him a big hug. 'Yes, that's my man. We got to stick together against these women folk.'

'Okay,' Karen said, 'everyone sit down. Let's pray and then eat. Who wants to lead grace?'

'I will.' David offered.

Taking each other's hands, they bowed their heads as David began.

As Karen listened to her son, her own thoughts turned to her own prayer of thanksgiving:

'Lord, thank you for blessing me with my wonderful family and helping me guide them to be the best they can be. As for Ivan, help him soften to the idea of our move so he can help me make this happen.'

As she was finishing her prayer, she heard her son call out her name.

'Mom? I said, Amen. You can let go of my hand now.'

'Amen!' she replied as she squeezed the hand of David on her right and Denise on her left. 'Let's Eat.'

Opening the bags, Ivan took out the dinners and set them on the table.

'This one's mine,' Ivan said, as he made a big deal of opening the container, much to the children's amusement. He was about to put in his fork to take the first bite when Karen asked if he was going to put his food onto a plate. 'No need, sis,' he laughed, 'It'll save on the dish washing. But I could use another fork.'

With a quizzical look, Karen walked across the kitchen to get him a fork from the silverware drawer before handing it to him.

'Not so fast me lassie,' he said in a pirate voice. 'This pirate captain needs a taster for his meal. I need to make sure you're not going to be poisoning me. Aaarrrrrr!'

As soon as his pirate voice came out, Denise started to giggle before they all burst into laughter.

'No chance of that happening captain,' Karen replied, as she took the fork back from him. 'I need your help to fix up this ship.' Then, taking some of the Egg Foo Young on the end of her fork, she brought it to her mouth and ate a bite to prove that his food hadn't been poisoned. 'See captain, no poison here.'

'Aye well, one can't be too careful. Aaarrrrrr!'

Ivan had the children laughing as they put their own food onto plates.

That evening, their Chinese dinner turned into a pirate feast, and it felt good to laugh. As Karen sat watching Ivan with the kids, she knew he had not done the pirate dinner sketch since they were little when she was having a hard time getting them to eat certain foods. Always at hand, Ivan would come over and play the pirate game to get the twins to hide the treasure. Convincing them that their food was the treasure, Ivan would get them to eat it up before the other crazy pirates would come to the house and steal it.

As the pirate dinner was winding down, Ivan brought up the subject.

'Well me mateys, your moms told me that you're all going to be off on an adventure soon. Moving your ship from this harbor down to the Plymouth harbor.'

'Are you worried about us moving?' Denise asked.

'Aye, who will I have my pirate dinners with?'

Denise just giggled.

'Mom loves this house,' David spoke up. 'Even though she's had a lady here looking at it, I can't really see her actually selling it.'

'We're definitely moving,' Karen said, as she looked at both David and Denise. 'You both met Daisy the other night when she walked through the house, and she gave me a list of what we need to do to get this place ready to sell. There were only three items on that list: fix the trim outside, paint a few of the rooms and declutter the house. There is nothing on this list that we cannot do. Especially if we do it together.'

'But Mom…' David tried to protest, before his mom raised her hand for him to stop and to let her finish.'

'We've talked about both of you going to college and becoming whatever, you want to become; a doctor, an accountant, a teacher or a lawyer. And you've both said that you want to go to college. Am I right?'

They both nodded in agreement.

'High school is a time when your studies become a little harder to prepare you for college,' she continued. 'You both know that I do my very best to give you both the best opportunities that I can, to make your dreams and futures as bright as they can be. Moving out to Plymouth, in the Wayzata school district, is so you will be able to attend a school that can prepare you for college in ways your current school can't. We're moving so that both of you can have the best future a mother can provide. That's why I asked Uncle Ivan over for dinner tonight as I want him to help us with the things, we cannot do by ourselves.'

Looking around the table she knew she had their attention. This was a pivotal time to get everyone on board. She took a deep breath and continued.

'Let me lay out the plan. May is our target to put the house on the market. Right before we sell the house we will move into an apartment. This way, no one will have to worry about keeping everything perfect for showing the house. With all our things moved, Uncle Ivan will have the time to come in and paint without anything or anyone getting in his way. It's not just Uncle Ivan's help I need, both of you are going to have to help me too.'

Both her children remained silent as they looked away from her and towards each other.

'I'm going to make you a deal. I know you like to spend Saturday's with your friends, but I need you to work with me on decluttering and packing up the house until three in the afternoon, only then can you go hang out with your friends. But this will be every Saturday until we're all packed up. Deal?'

Still looking at each other, the twins slowly nodded their agreement.

'My hope is that Daisy will find us a better house than this one. She found this one for us and it has been a great home. So, I know she can do it again.'

'Mom, can I ask a question?' David asked.

'Sure.'

'Will we be able to come back and visit our friends once we've moved?'

Karen reached out and took hold of her children's hands. 'Your true friends will still be your friends even if you move away. And we aren't going that far. So, I'm sure you will continue to see them, it just won't be every day like you do now. But in the summer, you all do so many different things it's not like you see them much anyway.'

Karen glanced over at Ivan and then back towards her children. 'As we only have about two months to get this completed, we need to get started tomorrow. Can I depend on you?'

Once again, they slowly shook their heads in agreement.

'May, I be excused?' David asked.

'Me too?' Denise added.

'Sure,' Karen permitted.

As they walked out of the kitchen David turned. 'Uncle Ivan, do you want to play my new Gran Turismo game?'

'I'll be right there.' he replied, with a reassuring smile.

Getting up from his seat, Ivan went over and sat next to Karen.

'Well sis, that went better than I thought it would go,' he said.

'It did,' Karen sighed, before turning to look at him. 'What was up with the pirate dinner thing?'

'You always had me do that with the kids when you wanted them to do something. I thought that was part of what I was supposed to do.'

Karen chuckled. 'I guess I did use you as the pirate a lot when the kids were young.'

'Yes, you did, and it always worked. So, I thought it might work this time too.'

For a few moments they sat in silence, listening to the twins talking upstairs.

'So, when do you think you can get to work on the house?'

'I haven't said yes yet?' 'Ivan replied, with a wry smile.

'Oh, yes you did.'

'When did I say yes?' Ivan demanded to know.

'As soon as you ate the dinner,' Karen laughed. 'Eating dinner was your implied agreement.'

'Aye lassie, you tricked me,' Ivan protested, in his pirate accent. 'I must go and walk the plank, or should I say race the plank?'

Getting up from his chair, Ivan kissed Karen on the top of her head as he made pirate sounds all the way up to David's room.

Alone, Karen began to clean up the kitchen, and as she lifted the plates her thoughts turned to prayer:

'Lord, I thank you for Ivan for I need his labor to get this house on the market. Thank you once again for my children for they have such sweet souls. I know this transition may be a bit rough but help them see the bigger picture and the amazing future that is in store for them. Help them to understand that everything I am doing is for their benefit. You are at the center in all of this, keeping everything in the right order. May I stay humble and be guided along the right path. I thank you for all the blessings you have bestowed upon us and for all the blessings you have planned for us in the future. May we be pleasing to you oh Lord, our Rock and our Redeemer. Amen.'

As Karen was praying, she felt like a weight was being lifted off her. A weight she had not realized was there. She replayed the evening in her mind laying out the moving plan and having everything out in the open brought a sense of relief. She could see God's plan unfolding and everyone was on board.

Chapter 3

EXPECTATION

*'Be anxious for nothing; but in everything by prayer
and supplication with thanksgiving let your requests
be made known to God.'*

Philippians 4:6

The morning came quickly, and Karen awoke feeling excited and had a sense of expectation of good things that were to come. Humming to herself in the kitchen, she had decided to make David and Denise's favorite pancake breakfast. The smell of the cooking was enough to bring them to the kitchen with smiles on their faces. She was so glad to see them.

Once they had finished eating, Karen turned to her plan of action.

'Okay, when I'm doing the dishes I want you two to go and get ready for the day. And I need you to make sure to come back down as we are going to start decluttering and purging this morning. Remember, it's just until three and then you can go hang out with your friends.'

It took her twins less time than she thought it would take before they were back in the kitchen, eager to begin.

'We're gonna start right away on decluttering the downstairs. Whatever apartment we move into is going to be a lot smaller than this house,' Karen reminded them before they got down to work.

It took three weeks to declutter the downstairs. During that time they had made great progress on the decluttering but not so much on the purging. By the fourth weekend they turned their attention to the bedrooms, and Karen knew that this would be the greatest test because this was *'their stuff.'* Soon the question of *'why do we have to get rid of our things, when we got rid of all that other clutter?'* Came from both David and Denise.

Karen had been expecting this subject to come up, so she was prepared for the question.

'First of all,' she began, 'we all have to get rid of things. Think of it as making your bags and boxes lighter so that we can take them to the apartment with us.'

The look on their faces said they weren't buying it.

'Tell you what we'll do,' Karen continued. 'Each of us will go to our rooms and find five things you no longer need and bring them down here. You have five minutes to decide. If you can't decide on what to take, then your sibling will go and pick something from your room. Okay? Go!'

As David and Denise hurried to their respective rooms, Karen went to hers. She had been thinking about what to get rid of and she already had a pile to pick from, so she was the first back to the living room where she took a seat on the couch and called out a two-minute warning. David was next to return with his items.

'Denise, do you need me to help you?' he heckled up to his sister.

A scream of '*no*' followed by, '*stay out of my room*' and '*mom*' filled the house.

'Well, get down here, you have thirty seconds before I send David up to help you.' Karen hollered back.

With a few seconds to spare, Denise came running into the living room with her items. The twins looked at what each other had brought from their bedroom.

'We're done now, right?' David asked.

'Not by a long shot,' Karen replied. 'First we are going to shift all of this out to the car. Only when the trunk and back seat are both full will we be done. This was only round one'.

'But we don't have that much stuff.' Denise said rather pleadingly, before turning to look at her brother.

'Oh, I think you'll be surprised,' Karen laughed.

After placing the first of their purged items into the car, they went back inside for round two of the five-item purge, and so it continued for a few hours. By the time they filled the car they were both amazed at the space they had in their rooms, in the hallway they high-fived each other, knowing they had accomplished something good together and somehow understood that by letting go of their stuff they had purged not only the "physical load" but some of the "emotional load" as well. Karen looked at the bright smiles on her children's faces and could not help but smile herself. She knew in that moment as they stood there that none of them had felt put upon that it was their *'stuff'* that had been purged.

'I'm going to take these over to the secondhand shop,' Karen said, lifting the keys of her car from the table in the hallway. 'Do you want to come with me, or would you like to take off early to go hang out with your friends?'

'Can I go over to JT's?' David immediately asked. 'He's got a new video game I want to try out.'

It only took a fractional nod of his mother's head before he was out the door.

Karen turned to look at Denise. 'What about you?

'Can I go over to Belinda's?'

'Of course,' Karen replied, as she hugged her daughter. 'Have a good time and I'll see you for supper. And thanks for all your help today.'

Later that afternoon, when Karen got back from dropping off all the items they had purged, she opened the door and looked around. Her house was looking so good and she knew it would not be long before they would be selling it. Yet, despite the days going by quickly, they still needed to get packed and moved into the apartment she had found for them so that Ivan could get in and do the painting and fix that trim.

Sitting down on the couch she made a call to Ivan. As the phone was ringing, she was betting that he would let it go to voicemail. To her surprise he answered on the fourth ring.

'Hey Sis. What's up? You inviting me over to dinner?'

'Sure, when do you want to come over?'

'How about tonight? I'm free tonight.'

'That's perfect, as I was wanting you to come over so you can see all the progress we've made. We can talk about the plan to get you in to do the painting and trim.'

'Already?' Ivan said, with a disbelieving tone.

'We've done so much purging and decluttering. The kids were surprised at how much space they have in their rooms. I was just admiring how big the living room looks,' Karen explained, before stating with great confidence, 'We're ready to start packing up our home.'

'This I gotta see,' Ivan chuckled. 'How about I bring over dinner tonight. Pizza Luce?'

'That sounds great. The kids will be home around six.'

'See you then.'

When David and Denise arrived home for supper, they noticed that the table was set but they could not smell any dinner cooking.

'Mom, who's coming for dinner?' Denise asked. 'The table's set for four'.

'Uncle Ivan will be here soon with pizzas, so go get washed up for dinner.'

'I bet we're having pirate pizza tonight.' David said.

'What's pirate pizza?' Karen asked.

'Well after the last time he was here, I bet he'll bring pizza and put on his silly pirate voice again.'

As Karen and Denise both began to laugh the doorbell rang.

'I'll get it,' Denise yelled, as she ran to answer the door.

'Who goes there?' she asked, in her best pirate voice as she stood with her hand on the door handle.

Aaaarrrrr!' came Ivan's reply from the other side.

In a fit of giggles, Denise opened the door and Ivan entered.

'Aye me mateys it's Captain Ivan and I've brought booty to share with ye all. I traveled far to the Isle of Luce to bring back their famous pizza pie.'

Taking the boxes from Ivan, David led everyone into the kitchen.

'Aye, there's the lassie that tried to poison me last time,' Ivan said as he winked at Karen. 'So, I thought I'd bring my own dinner for me crew.'

'Who me?'

'Yes, you lassie,' he replied, as he reached out and hugged her.

They all settled into their seats around the table and before anyone could open a pizza box Karen asked, 'Captain Ivan, as you've brought this bountiful feast for us, can you do the honors and lead us in the grace. But, please axe the pirate.'

Ivan smiled, they all held hands before bowing their heads and Ivan began the prayer.

'Lord, we thank you for this bountiful feast we are about to eat. Bless it to the nourishment of our minds and bodies. And all God's people said, Amen!'

A round of 'Amen's' came from the David and Denise. And then the pizza boxes were opened with a flourish.

'Thank you.' Karen replied as she looked over at Ivan. There was a look of relief on her face as she never knew what would come out of him, but that was part of his charm.

Dinner time passed quickly as the kids were always animated around Ivan. As dinner was winding down, Ivan brought back his pirate routine.

'Aye aye, me mateys,' he said, as he stood up from the table. 'It's now time for an inspection of the ship.'

Denise was giggling and Ivan looked at her through a squinting eye. 'It's no laughing matter lassie. We will start with your room. Come along Mateys.'

Up the stairs and to her room Denise marched leading the small band of pirates behind her. Upon entering she made dramatic hand and arm gestures to showcase the different areas of her room, looking like Vanna from her favorite tv show. For her grand finale she said, 'And behind this door, is the closet. See how roomy it is?'

Captain Ivan stepped inside to inspect it. 'Hmmmm' could be heard followed by, Bravo lass!' then he turned to David. 'It's your turn, Mate.'

Controlling his excitement, David led them across the hall to his room, and casually opened his door. 'Inspect away Captain Ivan.'

Ivan entered and looked around, hardly believing how empty the room was. He went to the closet and opened it. 'Impressive Lad'

Then turning around with a crooked smile on his lips, he looked at Karen. 'And lastly, your room me lass.'

Leading the way, Karen opened her bedroom door and stood aside.

Upon entering the room, Ivan could not believe the sight that met his eyes. No laundry, no ironing board, no piles of books peeking out from under the bed. He went over to the closet and it was half filled with hanging clothes and the other half was stacked with boxes. He looked over his shoulder to Karen with a questioning look.

'I've already started packing,' she replied.

Ivan immediately cut the pirate act. 'Everyone to the living room, it's time we had a family conference.'

Karen looked at him for some sign as to what he was thinking, but he just pointed the way to the living room.

When they were all assembled on the sofas, Ivan paced the floor in front of them. Karen felt a little alarmed and could not understand why he appeared so stern and had a puzzled look on his face.

Finally, he stopped in front of them and looked each one intensely in the eye. They were all on edge waiting for Ivan to speak.

He could hold it in no longer. Smiling and exclaiming, 'WOW! It's incredible! I can hardly believe my eyes. It makes me wonder what you did with my family. The Bonner family I knew liked clutter and stuff.'

Everyone could tell Ivan was teasing them and began to smile.

'We got rid of a lot of things,' Denise replied.

'I know Lass. I'm so proud of you.' Looking at Denise. Then looking around he said, 'I applaud you all. What a great job you've done. But you're not done yet.'

'What do you mean not done yet?' Karen asked, giving him a puzzled look.

'I mean you aren't done yet. You've got boxes to pack and a move to make before I can get in and paint. So, what is the timeline?'

'So, you think we did a good job on the decluttering and purging?' Karen probed with a smile.

'Most definitely. I hardly recognize the place. I never thought you'd do it. Now I want to get in here and paint, but I need it all out. So, what's the moving plan.'

'I get possession of the apartment on May first. I figured we could be packing boxes this weekend. Then I'll start taking things over in the car on the first after I pick up the keys. That weekend we'll move out most of the furniture. Daisy and I spoke about leaving a few pieces of furniture here, but she said to do whatever I wanted in the living room, but she'd like all the bedrooms clear.'

'Do we have boxes? We can start packing our stuff.' Denise said, getting rather excited.

'When do I need to have my PlayStation packed?' David asked.

'I'm glad you want to get started,' Karen replied, looking at them both. 'I've already got some boxes from the mailroom at the office and I was planning on getting more on Friday after work. We will start packing this Saturday morning. David if you want, you can save the PlayStation until last, but it needs to be packed by next Friday at the latest. I want everything packed but the clothes we will wear on the Saturday when we move.'

'Sounds like a great plan. I'll be here with a moving truck and I'll see about getting a couple of friends to help us move everything,' Ivan offered. 'But it all needs to be ready to go. The sooner we get you moved out the sooner I can get in and paint.'

'Uncle Ivan, do you want to play a few games before you go home?'

'Sorry David, not tonight buddy. I've got an early morning tomorrow. But I'll take a raincheck.'

'Let me walk you out,' Karen said.

Once they were outside Karen could not resist giving Ivan a big hug. 'Thank you so much Ivan. I don't know what I'd do without you.'

'I still can't believe the amount of stuff you got rid of, Sis. You've truly amaze me. Call me this weekend and let me know how you get along with the packing.'

'Will do. Be safe.'

Karen felt satisfied that they were right on schedule for Daisy to list the house in May. A few days later, Daisy dropped by with the paperwork for Karen to sign and a 'Coming Soon' sign to put in the yard. She was amazed when she saw the progress Karen and the twins had made.

'You really took to heart what I said,' Daisy remarked, as she walked around the decluttered house. 'I'm sure we'll have a buyer in no time. I'll bring over the actual 'For Sale' sign and place it out on the Monday after Mother's Day.'

'That sounds perfect Daisy,' Karen replied, knowing that all their hard work was going to pay off.

Everything was falling into place. Karen could hardly wait to see what Daisy would find them in Plymouth, but she knew in her heart it would be a wonderful house.

Next was step two of the plan - moving to an apartment until a house could be found. One might consider this move an extra step in the process, but Karen did not want to move into the wrong house. An apartment would give them time to find the right place. It would also allow for the twins to finish up junior high school without having to feel that they could not do anything in the house and mess it up. It also took the pressure off everyone for those potential buyer showings.

Every night, during her prayer time, Karen would pray:

'Lord, I know You will find us the perfect place to move to, but please remember to find the perfect buyer for

our old home. I know that Your timing will be perfect,
for it is written in Your word that to everything there
is a season and a time to every purpose under heaven.
Thank you, Lord, I can hardly wait to see what You
have instore for us. Amen and Amen.'

Towards the end of May, Karen received a call from
Daisy when she was finishing up work in the office for
the week.

'Karen, is this a good time to talk?'

'Hi Daisy, yes, you caught me before I started
home. What can I do for you?'

'Well, it's what I can do for you,' Daisy replied. 'I've
got great news! We have two offers on your house. The
first is at the list price, but they want a carpet allowance
of $3,000, for you to cover the closing costs, and for you
to provide a home warranty. They put down $250 with
their contract. The second offer is $15,000 less than
your list price, but they are not asking for anything and
they are already prequalified buyers. They put down
$1000 with their offer.'

'Wow Daisy you've been doing your job, not one
but two offers!' Karen said, as she sat on the corner of
her office desk. 'Daisy I know you can't tell me what
to do, but the first offer sounds like I'll be paying them
to buy my house. I don't understand how that works.'

'Karen the things that they are asking for we would
deduct from the price. So, you are looking at roughly
$7,000 - $7,500 off your list price. Money wise the
offers are about $7,500 - $8,000 apart. The biggest
difference is that the second offer, although it's less,

the buyers are already pre-approved on their financing. This will save time in the overall sale process. I don't like to present offers that have not been pre-approved for financing, but I also know you want the most for your home, so we have a good budget for your next home. The decision is up to you.'

'Daisy, this is great, can I give you my reply tomorrow? I'd like to think and pray about it.'

'Sure, we have twenty-four hours to respond.'

'Fantastic.'

'I'll phone you around noon tomorrow. Have a good night Karen.'

'You too Daisy. Goodbye.'

'Bye'.

Karen allowed the smile on her face to widen and looking up she began to thank God for not one but two offers on her house:

'Thank you, God, You are so good. I know the area I want to be in will be more expensive and I will need as much from the sale of the house as I can get. But Lord, having the pre-approval with the second offer I know there will be no delays because they already have their financing in order. Not that the good faith deposit matters, but offer one only had $250 and all those conditions, while offer two had $1000 down and no conditions. My internal feeling is offer one may look good for the money, but their intent seems to be getting as much as they can from me. But if they really want the house why would they not put more money down to show they were serious? Lord, the second offer, yes, it's a lot less, but I feel they are genuine with their

offer, no conditions and a serious good faith deposit. They just seem to be on top of buying a home with the financing already together. Lord, help me know in my spirit which is the best way to go. Thank you for listening to me Lord.'

After finishing work, Karen drove to her mother's to pick up the kids. The traffic was stop and go, but she still made it to her mother's in thirty-five minutes from downtown. She walked into the house humming and buzzing with excitement.

'Someone's had a good day,' her mother said. 'You're smiling and sound so happy.'

'I had a call from Daisy right before I left the office. She had great news on the house.'

'Did she find us a new house Mom?' Denise asked.

'Nothing about a new house yet but about our old house.'

'What about our old house?' David asked.

'Stop with all the questions and let your mom tell you all about it.'

'We have an offer on the house.'

Immediately, the twins started cheering and dancing around her.

'We actually have two offers on the table,' Karen continued, holding up her right hand to get them to calm their excitement so she could finish. 'I just need to figure out which one is the best for us.'

'Why don't I fix a celebration dinner?' Karen's mom offered. 'Then we can talk through the offers.'

'Momma, you know me too well,' Karen replied. 'I was hoping we could talk.'

'Yes, I've known you all your life and you're not one to make a decision without thinking it all the way through. Kids, why don't you go back and watch some T.V. while your mom and I talk and make dinner.'

As Karen began telling her mom about both offers her Mom started making the dinner.

'What is it that's making it difficult for you to make up your mind?' Karen's mom asked.

'Basically, even though I would end up with a better price with the first offer, there are so many conditions and their financing hasn't even been approved yet. With the second offer, I know that I'll end up with a lot less, but they are pre-approved, ready to go and there are no conditions.'

'Have you prayed about it?'

'Momma, you know I immediately went to God to ask his advice.'

'Keep listening Karen, you know God has always made a way for you and the children,' her mom said, as she reached out and gently touched her face. 'Sometimes, when I didn't think things would happen, you always believed that they would, and they did. Your faith is strong. Trust in Him. Just make sure it's His will and not your own.'

Throughout the dinner, on the drive home and as she put her children to bed, Karen kept pondering her mother's words: *Make sure it is His will and not your own.*

And so, that was the prayer she brought to the Lord as she went to bed. Despite handing it over to Him, she had a restless night.

Earlier than usual, Karen got up and started her day with her devotion time. The scripture that morning came from Proverbs 3:5-6.

> *'Trust in the Lord with all thine heart and lean not unto thine own understanding. In all thy ways acknowledge him, and he shall direct thy paths.'*

It was followed by a short prayer which Karen read, but she could not connect with what was written in the devotional booklet. Karen reread the bible verse and then went on to have her own conversation with Jesus:

> *'Jesus, this is one of my favorite verses and I know it by heart. I try to always acknowledge You and praise You for all You do and have done for me. I include You in all my decisions, because when I'm leaning on my own understanding things just don't go very well. But I don't understand why this is my devotion scripture for today. I was hoping today's scripture would be the word I needed from You to help me with my decision for the house. Lord open my eyes and let me see what I need to see in this scripture. Lord open my ears to hear what I need to hear today, and Lord give me a better understanding to better apply this to my life if I have been doing it wrong.'*

In the stillness of the morning Karen continued to remain in silence, waiting for the Holy Spirit to bring her to an epiphany, but nothing came her way.

Thirty minutes later, she looked over at the clock and saw it was time to get the morning going. It was going to be a busy day ahead. An hour later she had the kids up and ready to go out the door. After dropping them off at her Mother's she then headed downtown to work.

Once in the office, Karen focused on her job. The morning went by quickly. It was eleven-thirty and she knew she was going to have to talk to Daisy at noon. Collecting her thoughts, she began to pray again:

'Lord I feel like I'm at the Red Sea with Moses and Pharaoh's army is coming at me.' As she sat there the scripture from this morning's devotional kept coming to her mind. *'Lord what is it that I need to know?'* The phrase, *'lean not unto thine own understanding,'* kept reverberating in her spirit.

Shortly before noon, the phone rang, bringing Karen back to herself. As she answered the phone, she could see that it was Daisy by the caller ID.

'Hello, this is Karen.'

'Karen, it's Daisy. I'm calling to see if you've made a decision on the offers.'

'Could you please go over the offers with me again. I want to make sure I understand each one completely.'

Daisy went through both offers one last time.

'I know I'm going to need all the money I can get from this sale to cover the move out to Plymouth so we can afford a house there.' Karen explained, and the scriptural phrase *'lean not unto thine own understanding'* came to her again. Suddenly, without any doubt, she knew immediately which offer to take as a calmness came over her that sealed the decision she was going to make. 'Daisy let's go with the lesser offer.'

'You do know that the houses are more expensive in Plymouth? Are you sure you don't want to go with the higher bid?'

'Yes, I understand, but the lower bid is fine,' Karen said confidently. 'I know you will find us a perfect house.'

When the call was finished, Karen sat back in her office chair, and mentally she checked off selling the house on her to-do list, at peace that they were totally on schedule for moving to Plymouth. She knew there would still be a process to go through, but with the buyer having a loan pre-approved she knew it would be a smoother journey. Closing her eyes, Karen thanked God for not letting her lean on her own understanding.

A peace came over her and she could feel the Holy Spirit filling her heart. She knew God was well pleased. The plan was unfolding as He had planned for her.

Chapter 4

MILESTONES

*'My foot has held fast to His steps; I have kept His
ways and not turned aside.'*

Job 23:11

ime flew by, and before Karen knew it, June
had arrived and with it the twins' eighth grade
graduation; a milestone in their lives. So, Karen decided
to throw a small party for her family and their school
friends to celebrate their achievement.

As the party got underway, she stood to the side
and watched the interactions, taking great delight in
seeing the smiles and the fun. Both David and Denise
enjoyed every moment. Karen felt so proud of them,
but she knew that tonight's party marked the end of
their life in the city and the beginning of a new chapter
for her family as they moved out to the suburbs.

Many thoughts crossed her mind that evening, especially as to how the twins were going to make good friends once they moved to Plymouth. In that moment she felt a pang of guilt as she stood there. Feeling that her spirit was being brought low, Karen immediately cast such a thought aside, trusting that if their friends were meant to stay in their lives then it would be so, after all, they were not moving across country, just out to the suburbs. But she knew that going to a new school would be a challenge for them in trying to make new friends, especially as good friendship circles would already be established in their new school. She breathed deeply, for it would take some time and a lot of effort, but at least the twins would have each other. They always had a close relationship, and with that belief she cast her worry of them making new friends at their new school onto the Lord. For He was their Way Maker and she trusted that He would make a way for each of them. He was their Jehovah-Jireh, their provider.

Karen shook her head as she came back into the present moment and looked over at the twins smiling and thanking the Lord:

> 'Lord, this is a happy day for my family. I thank you for helping us make it through the eighth grade. I trust in your promises that you have great things instore for my family. Help us walk forward in Faith and not in fear. You are our Rock and Redeemer, our Jehovah-Jireh. Thank You for always providing for us, as only You know how. Amen.'

With graduation behind them the 'new' summer routine began with Karen going to work and the kids going to Karen's mom's house during the working day. For the first couple of mornings the twins complained that they were not getting to sleep in. Soon they realized that the drive from their new apartment to their grandmother's house was in the opposite direction from the way their mom needed to drive to work, which meant that after dropping them off Karen would have to backtrack her journey and then join the morning commute to make it downtown to work. Quickly, they all adjusted to their new schedule and things were working out.

Karen made sure she was always on time for work, so she had allotted a bit more time than needed in the mornings knowing that Minneapolis traffic was unpredictable, and she did not want to chance things. She wanted no special treatment from her boss. After all, it was her decision to move further away from the office and she knew her boss would accept no excuses.

Although moving to the suburbs was the right move for Karen and the kids, it was also a bit of a sacrifice for Karen. The length of her journey added twenty minutes to her commute, making it roughly fifty minutes each way. Yet, Karen was happy to have the extra drive time as it gave her a little more time for her morning conversation with God. Her car had become her sacred space. Time spent with the Lord was cherished by Karen, for she knew that the days when she did not have that conversation, that those were the days when things did not go as smoothly. With the

Lord at the wheel of her life, she trusted in His rhythm and knew that He would make her journey smooth and bring to her life a peace the world could never give.

Karen had a good job and knew she could transfer to a closer branch office if she requested it, but she loved working for Carol as she was a kind and fair boss. It was a respect that ran both ways and it was the biggest reason Karen did not mind driving the extra time to work.

Carol thought the world of Karen as she was one of the most conscientious workers she had as she was dependable, reliable and had an integrity in all her dealings with co-workers and clients. She had a great work ethic and never took time off unless David or Denise were sick, and those days were very rare.

When Carol heard that Karen was thinking of moving to the suburbs, she was a little worried that a transfer request would be forth coming. But the request never materialized. She was relieved when Karen sat down with her and told her about the upcoming move, reassuring her that adding time to the commute was a small sacrifice to make in order to stay in a good working environment. Mutual respect was key in the relationship between them both, and it grew deeper that day.

Since starting at the financial institution where she worked, Karen had advanced rapidly. In early June, she was even given the added responsibility of having a direct report, Linda. When Linda started to report to her, Karen knew favor was being given to her. The additional responsibilities at first were outside her comfort zone, but she thanked God for them and for the pay raise that came with the job. Karen knew that God's hands were involved in this promotion as she had asked Him in her prayer to make a way for her to afford the extra gas that would be needed by staying at the downtown location.

'Yes, thank you Lord for being my Way Maker.' Karen whispered, every time she recalled the blessings of this promotion.

Being a first-time manager was a little overwhelming and she wanted to be a good boss to Linda. So, Karen led by example, just as she had learned from her boss Carol, as she mentored Linda.

That summer, Karen knew that her work life was good and stable. Placing it into the hands of the Lord, was a blessing and a comfort to Karen for He was providing and taking away some of the financial challenges as His plan continued to unfold.

Chapter 5

NEW BEGINNINGS

*'Do not remember the former things, nor consider
the things of old. Behold, I will do a new thing,
now it shall spring forth; Shall you not know it?
I will even make a road in the wilderness
and rivers in the desert.'*

Isaiah 43:18-19

July had just arrived when Daisy stopped by to announce she had found them their new home. Daisy began to rattle off all its attributes as Karen reached out her hand for the listing. Immediately, a warmth and a knowing came over Karen when she looked at the picture and read the school district that it was in. All the details about this dream home created a fluttering in her stomach. She looked at the list price and her knowing feeling was confirmed.

This indeed was the one. She could feel it deep down in her soul. This was the one she had been waiting for. She was so excited that she began saying: *'Thank You Jesus!'* Over and over.

David and Denise heard their Mom and came running to find out what was going on. She showed them the listing and told them that Daisy had found them a new home.

'When can we see it?' Karen turned to Daisy and asked.

'We can go right now, if you like?'

With huge smiles of their faces, they grabbed what they needed and headed off to look at the house.

As they pulled up, Karen knew it was going to make the perfect home for them. As they began the tour, the twins went to explore the opposite way that Daisy and their mother went. Karen could hear them upstairs giggling and fighting over the bedrooms.

As she walked with Daisy through the main ground floor and as they entered each room, she could picture their furniture there and immediately saw everything had its place. This was the one. They went upstairs and joined the twins were they now took the role of a tour guide and showed their mom the different bedrooms.

'Mom come look at this room,' Denise said. 'This would be perfect for you and its right next to the bathroom.'

'It's nice but let's see the other rooms.' Karen replied.

'Oh Mom, you'll like this one better,' David chimed in with a big smile on his face.

As Karen walked in, she noticed it was decorated in more of a boy motif. It was about the same size as the last room.

'It looks more like you David. Let me see the last room.'

Entering the large master bedroom with its spacious en-suite bathroom and a walk-in closet, she turned and said to the twins. 'Now this is what I would pick for my room.'

Together they all burst into laughter.

As she watched them, Daisy felt a great sense of satisfaction that she had found the perfect home for this loving family.

As Karen drove the twins back to the apartment, she could not hide her excitement and the joy as to how God was providing for their needs just as He had promised. Knowing that this was the Lord's doing, she wasted no time, as her finances had already been pre-approved, Karen knew how much she could offer for the house.

Back in the apartment, she phoned Daisy and asked her to put in an offer. Daisy drew up the paperwork and later that day placed the offer - It was accepted.

The inspections and the loan paperwork were completed quickly, and the closing happened on July 31st. Everything was going like clockwork with moving day scheduled for August 15th.

Now moving into their new home and getting the home in order was her 'new stress.' When Karen started feeling stressed out, she would do two things: firstly, stop and settle herself by praising God and then praying, and secondly, break the project down into manageable steps.

During a daily devotion reading she brought her deepest feelings to prayer.

> *'Dear Lord, I know this is the right move for my family, but I am feeling anxiety and fear.'*

As soon as she had spoken her prayer, Joshua 1:9 was put in her heart. *'Have I not commanded you? Be strong and courageous. Do not be afraid, do not be discouraged, for the Lord your God will be with you wherever you go.'* Feeling fortified, Karen began planning the steps to make the move happen.

Her next step was to enroll David and Denise at the new school. When she first drove by the school, she could see that it was much bigger than their previous school. Immediately, the worry of them making friends and wondering if they would fit in, once again hit her spirit hard. But, just like she had done so many times in the past when even the tiniest bit of doubt or worry came to mind, Karen cast down the thought and started praising God with humming one of her favorite worship songs and prayed: *'Lord, take my doubts away. Help me keep to the plan and keep strong in Your ways, for I know this is Your will and it will be done. Amen.'*

Throughout, Karen kept herself calm and kept moving forward day by day, trusting that the Lord would get her through, just as He had done in the past. Daily she praised Him for all the goodness and opportunities He was blessing them with, and she prayed and asked Him to bless the kids with new friends.

With school starting in a couple of weeks, Karen once again picked up on the David and Denise twin connection during their evening meals. Just by looking at each other they were communicating without speaking and leaving her out of the conversation. She remembered when they were toddlers, it was like they had their own language and they could communicate. As they got older this communication was less vocal and involved more looks, like they were reading each other's minds. One evening over dinner, Karen asked them about it.

'It's hard to explain,' David shrugged.

'It's just like we can hear each other in our heads and have a conversation,' Denise answered for them both, 'but no one else, not even you mom, can hear.'

Karen remembered when the twins were about four or five, and she had taken Denise with her shopping. In the middle of the store Denise began crying and telling her mom they had to go home because David was hurt. Karen assured her that David was fine and that he was with their grandma. But Denise would not stop crying, so Karen hurried up with the rest of her shopping and they went right home.

On the way home, a fire truck and an EMT squad passed them. Karen did not think anything of it until she turned onto her street and could see that the fire truck was parked in front of her house. Denise started crying immediately and Karen hurried to stop the car. She had barely parked the car when Denise opened the door and jumped out, running into the house yelling for David. When Karen followed Denise, her mom met her at the door and was reassuring her that everything was okay before she could ask what was going on.

'David is stuck, and I couldn't get him unstuck,' her mom explained. 'So, I called the fire department.'

Karen remembered walking into the house and looking up at the top of the staircase, where on the landing David was stuck with his head caught between the spindles of the banister. As to how in the world it happened and as to why, she had no idea, but she felt somewhat reassured when she noticed that Denise went quickly to his side to reassure him that everything was going to be alright.

Over the passing of years, Karen often wondered how in the world did she know about David when they were away shopping. She often pondered on that special 'twin connection' that they always seemed to have had. She hoped it was a bond that would never end, and that it would always keep them close throughout life.

Their first day of high school was a big day for the Bonners. The typical pictures where taken that morning at home and then again at the school gates. The twins were so embarrassed, that Karen only snapped a couple pictures with the school as the backdrop.

Karen wanted to walk them in and take them to their classrooms, but she knew they were not in kindergarten anymore. Seeing that they were glancing around to notice if other students were watching, Karen knew it was time to let them go. So, she told them she would see them at home tonight as they would be riding the school bus home from now on. Taking a deep breath, the twins turned and walked toward the entrance, leaving Karen a little hurt that they did not give her a hug before they went in. But Karen, said nothing as she let them head to class. There at the gates she remained until she saw that they were both safely inside.

The twins were placed in separate homerooms, and that first morning was spent meeting their teachers and getting to know their way around the school during their freshman orientation.

That evening over dinner, Karen held her breath as she waited and prayed for a positive answer when she asked them how their first day had gone.

David and Denise started with 'their looks' and then started to talk about their day. They had the same lunch period, so they met up and had lunch together and talked about their classes. When she asked about the other kids, they replied 'there are lots of kids at this school compared to our old school. We don't know that we will ever really know people there.'

Those words cut at her heart.

'Well it was just your first day. I didn't expect you to be on a first name basis with everyone after one day.' Karen said; not sure if she was reassuring herself or her children.

The twins just chuckled at their mom's attempt to be humorous and continued eating. The evening conversations around the table went on this way.

Over the coming weeks, during her evening prayers, Karen prayed that God would bring David and Denise at least one good friend into their lives.

Each evening over dinner, Karen made a point to ask about their day and really listen to them. She knew moving out of the city was the right move, but she wanted more than anything for the move to become a positive experience for David and Denise, especially in their new school.

Two weeks into the school year and the routine, *'how was your day?'* conversation began when Karen realized that things had changed when both Denise and David started talking about their new friends. It was music to Karen's ears and an answer to another prayer. She smiled at her children and sat there praising the Lord in the depths of her heart for this blessing: *'Thank you Jesus for bringing these friends into their lives.'*

It was not long after that evening that Karen began getting to know the parents of Denise and David's new friends. It turned out they were good kids that came from good families. What Karen did not see coming and what turned out to be an unexpected blessing upon her life, was she started to become friendly with the mothers of these children. Another part of God's plan falling into place.

Chapter 6

UNEXPECTED BLESSINGS

'And God is able to bless you abundantly, so that in all things at all times, having all that you need you will abound in every good work.'

2 Corinthians 9:8

The first quarter of high school went extremely well for the twins. Even though their grades were average they appeared happy and were doing okay. They missed not being able to participate in some of the extracurricular activities, but they understood that money was tight. Karen hated having to tell her children *'no'* or *'not this year,'* but the budget just was not there, especially after having just moved. Karen was glad that the twins never complained, but in some ways that tore at her heart and was harder on her emotionally.

Sometimes bringing the doubt of was she being a good mother and provider for her children.

One evening, the mother of Denise's friend called Karen and asked if she was going to let Denise and David go to the Homecoming Dance. She explained that she hoped they were going because she did not want her daughter to be attending by herself.

'I don't know if they're going, they haven't really discussed it,' Karen replied, before asking for all the details the other mother was telling her all about the activities that would go on during the week. Karen quickly grabbed a pad and pen and jotted them down.

The following afternoon, as she was sitting in the breakroom having her lunch, she took out her personal planner and worked out her budget. The Homecoming Dance was only a few weeks away and she only had two pay periods to save some money for the twins to attend. No matter how many times she did the math, she knew she would not have enough.

When Debbie, her co-worker, entered to join her on her lunch break, Karen put the planner away and smiled at her as Debbie started talking about her cousin's wedding she had attended over the weekend. It was only as their lunch break was ending that Debbie complimented Karen on her jewelry.

'You have the best taste in jewelry!' she said.

'Do you really like it?'

'I do. Where did you get it?'

'I've had it for a while,' Karen replied, as a thought crossed her mind, a thought she at first dismissed but which she soon found herself sharing. 'Debbie, if you like it that much would you be interested in buying it?'

'Are you kidding?' Debbie cried, as her eyes lit up. 'I'd love to. How much do you want for it?'

'Make me an offer,' Karen said.

'How about $25 for the necklace and $15 for the bracelet?'

'Sold!' Karen agreed, with a grateful smile.

Both Debbie and Karen were excited, but for very different reasons. They decided they would wait until the end of the day to execute the transaction. This way Karen could finish the day wearing them.

At the end of the day they met up in the breakroom to make the exchange.

'This is great! I have the perfect outfit for it,' Debbie said, as she held the necklace over her neckline. Let me know if you have any other jewelry you're looking to part with.'

Karen was smiling, but the smile was not the bright happy smile she was known for. She knew this was an unexpected opportunity to bless her with some extra money. It really was a small sacrifice in the big scheme of things.

'I hope you enjoy wearing it as much as I have,' Karen replied. Then, not wanting to sound too eager, she added. 'Is there anything else that you've seen me wear that you'd like?'

'Well, there are a couple of other pieces that I simply adore,' Debbie confessed, as she described them to Karen.

Karen knew exactly which ones she wanted. As Debbie chattered on and on Karen's smile became a bit more plastered in place. One of the pieces David and Denise had had given her a few years ago and she knew she could not part with that one. But the others were ones that she had purchased herself. No real sentimental value there.

'I'll be happy to part with two of the three you mentioned,' Karen said a bit abruptly. 'The third one you described, well my children gave that piece to me, so I would not want to part with it. I hope you can understand'

Debbie completely understood and was excited to hear that Karen was willing to part with more of her jewelry.

'I'll bring in the other pieces for you tomorrow.'

On the way home, Karen thanked God, for sending Debbie her way today and giving her the idea and opportunity to make this extra money. Furthermore, she promised that on Sunday she would tithe on her extra windfall.

The next day after the other pieces of jewelry were sold, she pulled out her planner and started reworking her budget numbers. As a result of selling some of her jewelry and making a few savings here and there, Karen managed to pull together enough money for both David and Denise to go to homecoming all decked out in new outfits. She could hardly wait to surprise them.

The weekend before the homecoming she asked the twins about what was going on during the upcoming week at school.

'It's Spirit week and there is something special happening every day,' David replied.

'There's a pep rally, float building, a bonfire in the middle of the week, crowning of the Homecoming court, a parade Friday morning with the football game that night and a dance on Saturday night,' Karen added.

Denise was impressed that her mom knew the schedule for the week. She and David had decided not to talk about the festivities to their mom, as they didn't want to make her feel bad that they didn't have the money to go to some of the activities.

'Do you want to go to the festivities?'

'Mom we will go to the free events,' David replied. 'We know money is tight this year.'

'What if I had the money?' Karen asked, as she looked upon her twins with pride. 'Would you want to go?'

Immediately they both replied, 'Yes.'

'Well, I was able to pull some money together and I think we can get new outfits for each of you to go to the Homecoming Dance.'

'Really?' Denise asked, bubbling with excitement

'Yes, really!' We can go shopping tomorrow if your available.'

At first the twins struggled to find the words, but soon gave up when they realized their mom needed nothing more than a hug from them both.

What a great fall pick me up for all of them. It felt so good to surprise her children and see their delight. That evening once everyone was in bed and

Karen had finished her prayers, she laid there feeling pleased. Pleased that they were all settling into their new routines and lives here in Plymouth. As always, she gave God all the glory for making the plan and helping her execute the plan with grace and wonder.

Chapter 7

FROM OUT OF NOWHERE

*'Therefore, evil shall come upon you; you shall not
know from where it arises. And trouble shall fall
upon you; You will not be able to put it off; and
desolation shall come upon you suddenly,
which you shall not know.'*

Isaiah 47:11

*W*hen the homecoming was over the fall quickly
turned into winter and it was time for the kids
to take time off school for the winter break. This was
when life started to go downhill.

David, then fourteen years old, had just finished his
first semester of high school. He was a typical teenage
boy and a good kid. With the move out to Plymouth,
his first semester of high school had been tough, but
he had made two great friends; Quintin and Derrick.

Like most teens they loved playing video games, especially their favorites - NBA 2K and Madden NFL. By Christmas they had become true friends, and where you saw one of them you saw all three.

As the weather became colder outside, flu season raised its head. That winter break David took sick and at first everyone thought it was just a typical bad cold. For the first few days nothing appeared unusual, but David's cold started to get worse not better, and his coughing grew more intense.

Although David reassured his mom that he was fine, Karen knew this cough did not sound like any other cough he had ever had, for it sounded like it was coming from deep within his lungs. It hurt just to hear him cough. As a mother, Karen worried about him.

Since he was young, he suffered with asthma and it was always harder on him when he got a cold. Even though they had been through many colds that turned into bronchitis, his coughing had never sounded this deep nor lasted so long.

Call it mother's intuition, but Karen could just feel that something was wrong. At night when David would start coughing, Karen would pray: *'Lord, please touch David and give him the relief he needs to get some rest and get well.'*

Such prayers were usually followed with a trip to David's room, softly humming and going over to kiss his brow, checking for a fever, sometimes rubbing his back to sooth him. It reminded her of when he was a baby and the nights when she would walk the floor with him rubbing his back and humming to calm

64

him before he would fall asleep in her arms. Suddenly, another bout of deep coughing brought her back to the present and she knew it was time to get David to see a doctor.

When the morning broke, Karen got Denise up to get her ready for school. As she made her a lunch, Denise entered the kitchen as Karen was putting the breakfast onto a plate before setting it on the table.

'What's the occasion?' Denise asked. 'I can pour my own cereal.'

'I want to make sure you have a good hot breakfast,' Karen explained. 'It's cold outside and I do not want you getting sick too.'

'Mom, I'm fine.'

'I know, but I just want to keep you that way,' Karen replied, sipping on her coffee as she watched Denise eat her breakfast.

Later that morning, Karen called and tried to get an appointment with David's primary care physician, but to no avail. Everyone seemed to be sick and no appointments were available for weeks. Not being able to get to his regular doctor, Karen decided to take David over to the urgent care center. After waking him up, she poured him some hot tea and buttered him some toast to get his day started. She told him it was time to go see the doctor.

David, who hated going to see the doctors knew that he now needed one. So, after eating his toast and drinking some of his tea, he got ready and headed off with his mom.

After checking in, Karen could see that the waiting room was full. Even for urgent care the wait was going to be long. Thankfully, they were able to find two seats as a gentleman got up and moved to an available seat on the opposite side of the room so they could sit together. As worry swelled within her, Karen decided to hand her fears over to the Lord and bowing her head she quietly prayed:

> *'Lord I know you always tell us to give You our worries and fears for You will handle them. I know David is sick Lord and there are a lot of sick people in this waiting room. I want to pray for your blood to wash over David to keep him isolated from any of these other sicknesses in this room. I ask for your healing mercies for all that are waiting here today. Thank you, Lord. Amen.'*

After waiting for almost two hours, they were finally called to go in to see a doctor.

A nurse showed them the way to the examination room and asked David to sit on the exam table. After asking a few questions she took David's blood pressure and temperature. Once she was finished, she told them that the doctor would be right with them before she left the room and closed the door behind her, leaving Karen and David to wonder how long that would take.

'At least we're in an examination room,' Karen spoke to break the silence. 'I suppose that's one step closer to seeing the doctor.'

All David could do was just nod his head in agreement.

A few minutes later they heard the doctor entering the room next to them and greeting another patient. Then they heard the doctor leave and the door closing. The wait was agonizingly long as they heard the doctor enter four more rooms to see patients before he finally entered to see David. Reading the notes, the nurse had written on the chart, he walked over and stood beside David.

'Let's see what's going on here with you,' he said, setting the notes down on the edge of the bed.

Karen started to tell him about the cold and the cough and how seemed to be getting worse instead of better. Then, as she started to explain David's history of asthma, the doctor began to slowly shake his head as he continued with his examination.

Before she knew it, and having only looked into David's ears, nose, and throat the doctor turned to her and confirmed that it was just a bad cold.

'The boy should drink lots of fluids, to avoid becoming dehydrated, and get plenty of rest,' he said, writing something onto David's chart. 'There's nothing else we can really to do to fight a cold. I'll go ahead and prescribe something for that cough, and you can pick up the prescription from the nurse at the front desk.'

Then, as quickly as he had entered the room, the doctor left.

Karen was shocked that the examination had ended so quickly. Having been brought up never to question a doctor, she wondered if his diagnosis was correct. But who was she to tell a doctor he did not know what he was talking about?

After zipping up David's coat, before heading back out into the freezing cold, she stopped by the front desk to pick up David's prescription. She wanted nothing more than to get him back into his bed, and after making a quick stop at the drugstore, she drove him straight home.

There was no fight with him about just resting on the couch and watching television, and as she watched her son head straight to his bed, she knew he was a lot sicker than he looked.

As the days passed David's cough worsened which meant that he could not get a proper night's sleep, and then he completely lost his appetite. Those days were long, but the nights were longer as he struggled to get a comfortable rest. David could not be left alone, and when Karen had to return to work in the new year, her mother had to move in to watch him during the day.

When the school reopened, David was too sick to attend. On the first day of semester, Denise went to school by herself as Karen had to stay with David. It had been two weeks since they had been to the urgent care center and there was no sign of him getting better. Karen knew in her heart that this was way more than just a cold. It was getting worse. Every day she prayed for David to get better, but the harder she prayed the worse he seemed to get. Karen wondered if she was being tested like Job in the bible. Oh, how Karen wished that Pastor Bridges was still alive. He was one of the most treasured people that had helped Karen on her faith journey as a single mother. His mantra to her was engraved deep into her soul:

*'Child you just have to have Faith. And if you don't
think it's working, you have to look up and remember
Faith From a mother's soul moves mountains!'*

In that moment she knew, more than ever before,
that she needed to look up and remember where her
faith was from. She wanted God to know she put her
faith in Him and believed in His promises that He
would never leave or forsake her. But Karen also knew
that God would not do anything for her that she could
do for herself.

Enough was enough. As a mother she knew she
could no longer sit by and watch as her child lingered in
suffering. She was going to get him into see his primary
care physician. This was her mission of mercy for her
child, and she knew that she could let nothing stop her.

She called the doctor's office, but again she was
told that there were no appointments for at least two
weeks. They were prepared to place David on the call
list for any appointment that opened. That was all they
could do, and they promised to call the moment there
was a change in the doctor's schedule.

Hanging up the phone, tears came to Karen's eyes
as she bowed her head and began to pray:

*'Dear Lord, I thank You for all You have done and
provided for us Lord. We are happy to be in our new
home and for the friends that David and Denise have
made at school. Lord, I need Your guidance. I know
something is terribly wrong with David, but I just can't
seem to get him to see his doctor. Lord, I know You can
make a way for us. Please Lord make an appointment*

available, and if not, an appointment tell me what I need to do. Please Lord, give me Your guidance. I ask these things in Your mighty name. Amen.'

The moment she uttered the word *Amen*, Karen felt a calm came over her and the answer became clear in her mind. She would just take David to the doctor's office even without an appointment. The Lord would make it happen.

Chapter 8

ON A MISSION

*'Put on the whole armor of God, that you may be
able to stand against the wiles of the devil.'*

Ephesians 6:11

*K*aren's determination was at an all-time high.
She would get David into see the doctor, even
if it meant they had to sit in the waiting room the
entire day.

Phoning into work, Karen spoke with Carol her
boss and told her she was taking David to the doctor
and inform her that she would not be in that day. Then
entering David's room, she was shocked at how painful
it was for him to even cough. She knew this was no
seasonal cold for it was now getting worse by the
minute. After helping David to dress in several layers to
keep out the cold she managed to get him downstairs,

71

outside and into the car. With every movement she could feel his strength ebbing away.

The drive to the doctor's office seemed like an eternity as a feeling of urgency kept bubbling up inside her. With the bad weather, she worried about getting a parking spot, but as she turned into the parking lot there was a spot just waiting for her not far from the entrance. Praising the Lord for the spot as she pulled in, she knew it was a sign that He was making the way clear for David.

They were barely inside the door when the nurse took one look at David and could see that he was very ill. Looking into the computer there miraculously appeared an opening on Dr. Rogers schedule; David's primary care physician. Karen immediately started thanking God for making the way clear for David.

Once they were in the examination room there was a slight wait, before the nurse ushered in Dr. Rogers.

'What seems to be the problem, young David?' he asked, as he walked over to him.

David could hardly speak between the fits of coughing.

Karen started trying to explain but Dr. Rogers asked her to let David explain.

'David,' he continued, placing his stethoscope into his ears to listen to David's chest, 'how do you feel?'

'I feel awful,' David said, struggling for breath. 'I can't… stop… coughing.'

As the doctor continued to listen to his chest, David started to shed silent tears.

In silence Dr. Rogers continued his examination, taking David's temperature, checking his vitals, looking deep into his ears and throat before listening to his chest once again.

As Karen watched the doctor examine her son, she noticed how his facial expression became very stern as he listened intently to David's chest. Inside, she pleaded for God to make everything alright for her son and for Him to heal the suffering her baby was going through. *Just make him well Lord. Just make him well.*

After listening to his chest, Dr. Rogers immediately orders a series of x-rays of David's chest, explaining he needed to see what was going on inside as he did not like what he was hearing, especially the deepness of David's cough.

Unable to walk down to the floor below, the nurse wheeled David to the x-ray suite where the technician was waiting for them.

'Are you David Bonner?' the technician asked, as he took David's chart from the nurse.

'Yes,' he just about managed to reply.

'Let's get you on the mend, David,' the technician replied, as he took the wheelchair from the nurse.

Karen was about to follow them into the room when the technician instructed her to wait outside. Although she knew that x-ray suites only permitted patients, she felt annoyed that she could not stay with her son.

'I'll be right out here if you need me.'

Within seconds, the door to the x-ray suite was closed and Karen was left standing there, unable to do anything but wait.

There were a mixture of feelings that rushed through Karen: guilt that she hadn't been more forceful a few weeks ago with the urgent care doctor, helpless because she didn't know how to make it all better and scared that somehow, she would lose David. Immediately when the last thought registered in her conscious mind, she cast it down. As the time slowly passed, she felt her own emotions coming to the surface and tears began to leak out of her eyes.

Leaning back against the wall, she closed her eyes and prayed:

'Lord, I just want to thank You for making a way for us to get in to see Dr. Rogers. He knows David, and I just feel like he will know what is wrong. So, Lord I ask that You guide Dr. Rogers and give him the wisdom and know how to treat David. I ask this in Your mighty name. Amen.'

In that moment, she surrendered everything over to the higher power, knowing that the Lord would anoint David with healing from on high.

Hearing the x-ray door open Karen quickly wiped the tears away and was off the wall and right there surveying David from head to toe. Karen told the technician she would take David back upstairs. The tech asked her to wait a moment, she turned back to her desk, picked up the phone and called upstairs letting them know that David had finished his x-rays. She listened and then said, 'I'll bring him up.'

'I'll escort you and David back to Dr Rodgers office. This way you don't have to wait for a nurse to come down to get you.'

Karen knew it was procedure, but she wanted to be the one pushing the wheelchair not walking behind like someone in a parade. Inside she was crying out to the Lord: *'Lord, I know you are in control but it hard for me to let go. Help me to let go and let you take over. I know you have a plan, but I do not understand why David must be so sick and suffer. Please Lord make him well and help me to understand your plan for us.'*

Chapter 9

WHAT NEXT?

'I can do all things through Christ which strengthens me'

Philippians 4:13

Back in the doctor's office, the wait seemed like forever as David tried to get comfortable on the bed and fight the urge not to cough, while his mom could only watch on and pray for a quick return of the x-rays so that her child could be properly diagnosed and treated. The clock just kept ticking away the minutes as David and Karen waited patiently for over an hour for the results. Karen tried to keep it together and not show any fear or anxiety in front of her son, but she had this feeling that whatever was causing David to be sick, it was not good. As the wait went on, her uneasiness heightened. In her mind, she kept asking God to help keep her calm.

Meanwhile, outside in the waiting room, the x-ray technician had delivered David's x-rays; stating that Dr. Rogers needed to review them right away as a matter of urgency. The nurse, knowing that David was sounding worse in his coughing, knew something was seriously wrong and immediately took the x-rays and waited outside the examination room that Dr. Rogers was currently working in. When he came out, she handed him the x-rays and relayed the technician's concern.

Taking the x-rays, Dr. Rogers went directly to his office to view them in private before he went to see David and Karen. He had barely stepped back from putting the x-rays up when he immediately saw the cyst on David's left lung. It was the size of a half dollar. Having listened to David's chest he knew he had heard fluid building up in his lung. While pulling down the x-rays he asked his nurse to call for an ambulance and also call over to University Hospital to let them know he was sending David over, and then with the x-rays in hand he strode briskly towards the examination room where David and his Mother were waiting.

The moment Dr. Rogers abruptly entered the room, Karen knew that the news was not going to be good from the very concerned look she saw on his face.

'You are one sick young man,' Dr. Rogers said, as he walked over to David. 'I'm sending you to the University of Minneapolis hospital by ambulance. We have already called them, and they will be here shortly to take you over.'

The urgency and tone of the doctor hit Karen like a punch to the stomach. Her breath was almost taken away. 'What?... Why?... What's wrong?' she managed to gasp.

In response Dr. Rogers went over to the side of the room and put David's x-rays up on the illuminator and switched on the light so they could see them.

'I sensed, having listened to his chest, that he had fluid building up in his left lung,' he explained, as he took his pen out of his pocket and started to point towards the x-rays. 'Can you see, just here on David's left lung?' he asked, pointing at an area that looked like a solid white circle. 'It appears to be a cyst. This fluid is what is causing David's issues. I'm sending you right over to the hospital as we must get that fluid out of his lungs and get that cyst drained. By the color of the x-ray you can see the cyst is full of fluid, so we need to get it drained before it bursts. David's coughing is agitating it and makes it even more susceptible to rupturing.'

The moment David heard those words he was overcome with fear, and even though he was scared to cough he just could not stop the involuntary reaction to do so.

'It's going to be fine son,' Karen reassured him, stroking his hair when she saw the fear etched on his face.

One thing she knew for sure was that she was going to need help. So, lifting out her phone she told David that she was going to call Ivan to tell him what was going on. She knew if she did not call him right away, that he would be upset and this was not the time for discord in the family, for David needed all the support he could get right now. This time there was no going to voicemail as Ivan answered on the third ring.

'Ivan, I know you are at work, but please listen for just a minute,' she began. 'I'm at the doctor's office with David and he is very sick.'

'What's wrong with him?' Ivan asked, the panic clear in his voice.

'The doctor has called for an ambulance and we're being sent over to the University of Minneapolis Hospital.'

'What?'

'He's going to be fine,' Karen explained, not wanting to panic Ivan nor David any further. 'I just need you to meet us there.'

For a few moments, Karen walked away from David so he could not hear what his uncle was saying.

'Okay,' Karen finally spoke, 'just get there when you can.'

'Is he coming?' David managed to ask.

'Yes. He has a few things to finish up and then he will be there.'

Yet, inside Karen was praying to the Lord that Ivan would make it to the hospital sooner rather than later as he was working on a job over twenty miles away, and with the snow she knew it would take him some time.

Minutes later, the nurse knocked on the door and informed them that the ambulance had arrived. Soon, two paramedics, Nancy and Ted, came in with a stretcher, seeing that David was so weak they lifted him from his bed rather than getting him to stand.

'David, just try to relax,' Nancy said, as she placed a blanket over him before strapping him in.

As hard as he tried, David could not stop coughing, and when he laid flat his coughing became uncontrollable.

Immediately, the nurse stepped in and instructed the paramedics to raise the upper part of the stretcher to help ease his discomfort.

'Does that feel any better?' Nancy asked, as she raised the stretcher.

Although David was still coughing, he did not feel as uncomfortable, and was able to nod at Nancy.

As the paramedics rolled David out of the examination room, the nurse handed Karen some paperwork to take with her to the hospital. Then walking beside the stretcher, she held David's hand and kept reassuring him that everything was going to be all right. She could tell he was scared and anxious. She knew she had to keep it together and to remain calm.

Once the paramedics got to the ambulance and opened the doors ready to place him inside, Karen did the only thing she could, and that was to bend down, to kiss his forehead and to tell him that she loved him. With those words of love spoken from the heart, the paramedics placed the stretcher inside the ambulance.

As Nancy climbed up beside David, Ted closed the doors and went around and got into the driver's seat while Karen made a mad dash to her car to follow right behind the ambulance.

With the sirens blaring to get them through the Minneapolis traffic, Karen remained right on their tail for she was a mother on a mission. When the ambulance drove through the red lights, she drove through them as well.

Inside the ambulance, Nancy could tell that David was scared as he kept looking around him; the fear clear to see in his eyes.

'I know the sirens are loud,' she explained, 'but we need them to get through the traffic.'

Throughout the ride she talked to David in a calming voice as she kept monitoring his vitals.

'David, do you like sports?' she asked, trying to distract him from everything that was going on.

'Football... Basketball.'

'A Timberwolf fan?' Nancy jumped on the topic trying to relax David, but David was too distracted trying to look out the rear windows.

'Don't worry your mom is right behind us,' she reassured him. 'You gotta hand it to your mom, she sure can drive. Was she ever a racecar driver?'

David smiled and shook his head no.

'All I can say is she must be staying up late at night playing Need for Speed or that Indy 500 race game.'

David started to laugh which only started coughing spell.

'I won't make you laugh anymore. Just know your mom is right behind us just like she promised.'

As she drove behind the ambulance, Karen prayed like never before:

'Lord, please Lord, help my David. I know if I have faith the size of a mustard seed You will hear

my prayers. My faith Lord is much bigger than the mustard seed, so I know You must be hearing me. Lord, let no weapon formed against him prosper. I'm asking for Your divine healing. Lay Your healing hand on David. God, I know You got this. I just want to make sure You got this. I know I must give it to You, but he's my baby. You entrusted him into my care. But we need Your divine healing. Please Lord, help us get to the hospital without incident. I'm praying all of this in the mighty name of Jesus. Amen.'

With the winter weather it took nearly 30 minutes to get to the hospital. With the main hospital entrance only allowing ambulances, Karen had to bypass the entrance and go straight to the parking lot. She knew God was making a way today when she saw a free parking spot not far from the entrance. Karen parked, got out of the car and made it back to the ambulance as David was being unloaded.

She grabbed David's hand and squeezed it to reassure him that she was there. She could tell by David's eyes that he was happy to see her even if he did not have the strength to say anything. She stayed right alongside the stretcher as it was wheeled into the emergency room.

When the paramedics got David into a side room, they lifted him and placed him onto an emergency room gurney as a nurse approached to get some information and the paperwork from Karen. Karen tried to explain all that had happened as she found the paperwork in her purse to give to the nurse. The nurse on duty had already spoken to Dr. Rogers and knew how serious David's situation was.

Soon, a flow of doctors and nurses began entering and exiting the room. They drew blood samples and sent them off as well as checking David's vitals.

Throughout, Karen just kept praying over and over to herself: *'Lord heal my David.'*

Within an hour, the senior emergency room doctor entered the room.

'You know there is a cyst on David's left lung,' he spoke directly to Karen as she stood alongside David. 'We're going to have to go in and drain it, because if it bursts there would be serious complications from the toxins spreading throughout his body and a chance of the lung itself collapsing. We will have to perform surgery to do this, so we need to plan the day and prep David for the procedure. We are working to get our team in place. We have given David a little something to help him relax and rest.'

Even though David was still coughing a little, Karen could see that he was leveling out. Kissing him on the cheek she told him that she was going to step out to the bathroom and make a call, but that she would be right back.

He managed to nod his head in acknowledgement.

Karen knew this was major and that she needed to get prepared as well. On her way to the restroom she spied a small waiting room across the hall. As the small room was empty, she stepped into the waiting room and closed the door to make her call to the office. Contacting Carol her boss to request a leave of absence from her job was her order of business, for there was no way she was going to be leaving David alone in a hospital.

Carol picked up immediately, Karen explained the situation and asked what she would need to do to take a leave of absence. Carol was very accommodating and advised she would get in touch with human resources to find out what needed to be done and would let her know. She also told Karen to keep her informed-on David's situation, and if there was anything, they could do for them to please let her know. Karen sighed with relief that the call went so smoothly. It was wonderful to have a boss that was compassionate and willing to work with her during this difficult time.

Karen had not seen Ivan come into the hospital yet, so she quickly placed a call to him. It went straight to voicemail.

'Hey Ivan, we are here at the hospital in the emergency room area waiting for a room for David. I know you'll get here when you can. Be careful with the weather. See you soon.' Karen disconnected hoping that her message sounded lighter than she felt. She headed back to David's small examination room in the ER. As she walked in there were a few more nurses with him taking vitals yet again.

From the time they got to the emergency room it took four hours before they had a bed ready in the intensive care unit for David. Once in the room, they got David into a gown and settled him in. 'Is he alright?'

Turning around, Karen was relieved to see Ivan walking towards her. With her emotions running high, Karen immediately walked over and hugged him.

'Here, here, sis,' Ivan whispered, as he wrapped his arms around her. 'Everything is going to be alright.'

Karen replied with silent tears.

'So, young man,' Ivan said, as he walked over to David's bed, 'How's you?'

David tried to reply, but immediately started coughing.

'David's left lung has fluid in it, and they have found a cyst,' Karen explained, as she took her son's hand. 'We're waiting for a surgeon to come in and explain what's going to happen next. All we can do now is wait and pray.'

Ivan pulled a chair over by the bedside so that Karen could sit down. He moved to the chair that was at the end of the bed. Nurses came in and out of the room checking on David. Both Ivan and Karen became lost in their own thoughts as they sat there waiting for a doctor.

Karen kept replaying the events of the day in her head. She was having a hard time understanding why David? Why now? It brought to mind a passage in Luke 2:35 *'a sword will pierce through your own soul also, that the thoughts of many hearts may be revealed.'*

Karen wondered if this was how Mary felt about Jesus as she watched the rejection and pain of his crucifixion. Seeing David like this did pierce her heart all the way to her soul. But how is all this part of His plan for us?

Chapter 10

AND THE DRAMA BEGINS

'For we walk by faith, not by sight.'

2 Corinthians 5:7

*A*midst all the frantic worry and activity at the hospital, Karen realized it must be about time to pick Denise up from school.

'I've got to go pick up Denise at school,' Karen said, as she glanced at her watch. 'Ivan would you mind staying with David until I get back?'

'Of course,' Ivan replied. 'You go do what you need to do. I'll watch over your boy.'

'I'll be back shortly,' Karen said, as she kissed David's forehead. 'I love you. Take care while I'm gone.'

'I... love you... too,' David whispered.

Karen left Ivan with David and departed the hospital.

Karen did not want Denise taking the bus home and to arrive at an empty house, as she was not sure how long she would have to stay at the hospital. Karen thought it would be good for David to have his twin by his side as their connection was so tight it would be extra support.

As Karen drove up to the school, the buses were just starting to line up.

'*Good*,' she thought, '*I made it before she got on the bus.*'

Karen parked the car and started towards the school just as the closing bell rang and the doors opened with a steady stream of students flooding out.

When she saw Denise, she started to wave.

'Mom, what's wrong?' Denise asked, surprised to see her there.

'Nothing's wrong. Why would you think that?'

'Well you don't usually pick me up from school and when I left this morning you were with David. Is he okay?'

'It's cold out here. Let's get in the car and I'll tell you all about it.'

Placing an arm around Denise's shoulder, Karen headed back towards the car. Denise tried to ask questions, but Karen said in a direct no-nonsense reply that they needed to keep moving.'

This was not like her Mom. Denise knew something was up.

'Mom tell me what's wrong?' Denise asked, the moment they were both inside the car.

'Let me get out of the school lot and I'll tell you on the way,' Karen replied. 'And while I'm doing that, tell me about your day.'

Hesitantly, Denise started telling her mom about her day, all the while knowing that something was not right.

As Karen turned her car onto the street, she knew she only had a few minutes to collect herself before telling Denise about David. Her mind wrestled between listening to Denise and praying: *'Oh Lord, what am I going to say so I don't scare Denise or upset her about David? Please Lord, give me the words.'*

Denise knew her Mom was not really listening to her as she appeared lost in her thoughts. Then, when they got to the main street that would take them home, instead of turning left her Mom turned right. Something was wrong. Denise raised her voice and tugged on her Mom's arm like she did when she was little.

'Mom, are you listening to me?'

'Yes,' Karen replied.

'You can't be,' Denise replied, rather frustrated. 'You just turned the wrong way to go home.'

'I know,' Karen said, as she gripped the steering wheel. 'I need you to listen for a bit while I drive and talk, okay?'

'Okay.'

'After you left for school, David sounded bad, so I phoned into work to take the day off to take care of him. I decided he needed to get into see Dr. Rogers, so I took him over to his office and we were able to get in to see him. Dr. Rogers didn't like the way he was coughing so he took some x-rays and he found out that David has a cyst on his lung, and it has filled with fluid. So, he sent us over to the hospital. I called your uncle Ivan and he came over and is staying with David while I went to pick you up. I didn't want you at home by yourself as I wasn't sure when I'd get home. And I didn't want you to worry so I thought it would be good for David to have us all there with him. You know, for support.'

'David's in the hospital?'

'Yes,' Karen answered.

'So, what are they doing to him?'

'They're going to have to...' Karen choked on the words as tears welled up in her eyes. Reaching across the seat she took hold of Denise's hand. 'They're going to have to operate on his lung.'

As her daughter broke down crying, Karen, through her own tears, reassured her that everything would work out fine as David was in the Lord's hands.

For the rest of the journey to the hospital, Karen drove on auto pilot. Soon they turned the corner and saw the hospital come into view. Parking this time was a challenge, so they circled a bit and then found a spot. Before, they got out of the car, Karen reached over and took Denise's hand once more and squeezed it.

'I love you.'

'I love you too, Mom,' Denise replied.

Getting out of the car, they walked quickly to the hospital. The temperature was dropping outside, and now a cold wind was blowing. Entering the hospital, they were glad to feel the instant warmth and it felt good to be inside.

Knowing the room David was in, Karen did not have to stop by the reception desk, and she led Denise straight over to the elevators. The lobby was busy, and people were waiting at the elevators. Two elevators arrived at the same time. The one nearest to them had quite a few people exiting, so they stepped aside. The other elevator was empty and everyone else filed into it. Karen was kind of glad that no one else decided to ride her elevator as she was not in the mood to be surrounded by a lot of people.

Finally, Karen and Denise entered the empty elevator. Just as Karen pressed the button for the sixth floor, two other people joined them.

'Which floor?' Karen asked.

'Four, please,' the gentleman replied.

Karen smiled and pressed the button for the fourth floor. As the elevator ascended, Denise kept looking down at her shoes trying not to fidget. The couple did not even seem to notice that Karen and Denise were there as they were so into each other, holding each other's hands and smiling. The elevator came to a stop and there was a ping as the doors opened to the fourth floor. Karen could see it was the maternity floor. Guessing by the look of the couple they were going to be new parents. Karen remembered those happy days when she found out she was going to have twins.

The couple exited, leaving Karen and Denise to ascend the last two floors. The elevator stopped and like before a ping sounded as the elevator doors opened.

They exited the elevator and Karen started to lead the way down the corridor.

'Mom, are you sure we're on the right floor?'

'Yes, why?' Karen replied.

'This is the ICU floor.'

'I know honey, David is just down the hall.'

Denise had not been to many hospitals before, let alone to an ICU floor. She could not believe that David was so ill. Her senses were on heighted alert and when Karen looked at her, she looked like she was getting ready to go into the fight or flight mode; leaning more towards flight. So, Karen reassured her that everything was fine as she took hold of Denise's hand, so she would not bolt.

'He's right down here at the end of the hall. And your uncle Ivan is here too. It's fine, come on, David will be happy to see you.'

As they made their way down the corridor, Karen steadied herself as she did not want to upset Denise anymore. But as they rounded the corner and entered David's room, her world collapsed around her when she saw that David was on a ventilator.

She did not know what to say or do. She just stood there, frozen with Denise squeezing her hand. She looked over at Ivan, but he just sat there looking at David.

David was lying there on a ventilator and tubes appeared to be coming from everywhere. Karen once again looked over at Ivan, who just sat with a stunned, blank look on his face.

'What has happened to my baby?' she finally managed to ask.

The nurse insisted that she needed to get the doctor She skirted around Karen and Denise and was out the door. Karen let go of Denise's hand and walked over to the bed and held David's hand. Denise not knowing what to do just moved over to the side of the room like she was trying to blend into the wall. There was a straight-backed chair there that she just sat on. Surveying the room looking at her uncle and then back and David and their mom. All she could think was this is a bad dream.

It wasn't long when the nurse returned with a doctor. 'Mrs. Bonner, I'm Dr. Mumford.'

'What in the world has gone on here?' Karen asked. 'David was fine when I left to go pick up my daughter from school and I come back to this?'

'I understand,' Dr. Mumford replied. 'Let me tell you what has transpired since you were gone. As we mentioned we were going to prepare David for theatre. We needed to perform an endoscopy so we could see what was going on with him before we operated. As we were trying to put the scope down his throat, David coughed, and the cyst burst, and the poisons went through his body. The good news is that David's lung did not collapse as that often happens if a cyst bursts. We have heavily sedated him, so he is in no pain now.' The doctor could see the worry grow in Karen's eyes. 'Understand, David had to be intubated to draw the poisons out of his body. For David to recover, the poisons have to be removed.'

Karen felt sick to the pit of her stomach as she looked at all the tubes. The tubes that were being used to flush out the infection drained into what looked like canisters which were filling up with hazardous wastes coming from David's body.

'This entire process is going to be lengthy,' Dr. Mumford continued, 'and the body has to withstand this method of treatment. David is young and strong which is all in his favor. Older patients' bodies cannot always tolerate this process and do not recover. This is a serious situation.'

'I understand,' Karen murmured, but she did not understand at all.

When the doctor left, Karen went over and stood in front of Ivan so he would have to look at her.

'Ivan, what happened?' she asked in a stern voice.

'I don't really know,' he said as he began to cry. 'It just happened so fast and people were running in here to help David and I was pushed over here in the chair out the way. Karen, I don't know what to tell you. There was nothing anyone could do.'

In that moment, Karen knew what she had to do. Turning to David she took hold of his hand, closed her eyes and prayed:

'Dear Lord, thank You for blessing me with both David and Denise. When the doctors told me, I would never have a child, you told me you would make me a mother and You blessed me with two children not just one. You told me that my children would grow up to become a mighty man and woman of God. Lord, I don't understand what is happening with David. How could he be struck down to this? I was only gone a little

over an hour. Lord I don't understand what happened, but I do understand that You are the Master Physician and there is nothing bigger than You. Lord, I am walking in Faith of Your promise given to me so many years ago. So, Lord, I don't know how, but I know You are going to heal my David. And I thank You in advance for that my Lord. Amen.'

As Karen finished her prayer, she turned around to see Denise and Ivan, both with big eyes, just looking at her and David. They all just looked at each other. No other sound, other than the ventilator that was attached to David, could be heard in the room. Then as if on cue to enter and break the silence Dr. Rogers entered the room.

'How is David doing?'

'He was fine when I left to pick up Denise and I came back to this,' Karen replied, extending her hand towards David. 'You tell me how he's doing?' Karen moved out of the sightline of Dr Rogers so he could see David on the ventilator.

The moment Dr. Rogers saw David he was shocked, then looking at Karen he said, 'Let me look at his chart and I'll check his vitals myself and I will track down Dr. Mumford and get some answers.'

Karen cooled a bit. She knew it was not Dr. Rogers fault, but she needed to understand what had transpired after she left.

Chapter 11

STAND ON HIS WORD

*'You are My battle axe and weapons of war: for with
you I will break the nations in pieces;
with you I will destroy kingdoms.'*

Jeremiah 51:20

Karen had close friends from her church and work praying for David. Every day she went to the hospital, bringing a cassette player into the intensive care room, where David was sleeping and receiving treatment. David had been heavily sedated and put under an induced coma. Even though he did not realize that his mother was with him, Karen, being faithful to God, prayed, sang and talked to him constantly. And when she was not singing and praising the Lord or praying, she was reading the Bible to David.

One of his favorite stories growing up was David and Goliath. Especially the part where David went out to face Goliath in the First Book of Samuel:

> *Meanwhile, the Philistine, with his shield bearer in front of him, kept coming closer to David. He looked David over and saw that he was little more than a boy, glowing with health and handsome, and he despised him. He said to David, 'Am I a dog, that you come at me with sticks?' And the Philistine cursed David by his gods. 'Come here,' he said, 'and I' ll give your flesh to the birds and the wild animals!'*
>
> *David said to the Philistine, 'You come against me with sword and spear and javelin, but I come against you in the name of the Lord Almighty, the God of the armies of Israel, whom you have defied. This day the Lord will deliver you into my hands, and I' ll strike you down and cut off your head. This very day I will give the carcasses of the Philistine army to the birds and the wild animals, and the whole world will know that there is a God in Israel. All those gathered here will know that it is not by sword or spear that the Lord saves; for the battle is the Lord's, and he will give all of you into our hands.'*

After reading this passage, Karen spoke into David's ear:

> *'My son you are David. You are a fighter and blessed by God. Your Goliath comes at you with sickness and poison but you David come against this sickness in the name of Jesus, the Lord God Almighty. Remember*

the battle is the Lord's, let Him deliver you from this sickness.'

It was times like this that she felt the presence of the Lord in the room, wrapping her and David in love and healing.

Karen knew she had to keep the Word of God in David's room and keep the naysayers and negativity away from him. As the days turned into weeks, Karen's faith was constantly tested by the people closest to her. She expected that kind of behavior from Ivan but not from her friends and even her pastors. The people that had supported her in times of trouble just did not seem to be there for her in this time. Even her own mother had her moments, but in the end, she always came back to support Karen and her steadfastness in faith.

It was during the third week that David was at his lowest in the opinion of the doctors. The doctors called a meeting, it was Ivan and Karen with the doctors. The doctors kept explaining the seriousness of the situation and that they could not see any improvements in David's condition. They advised that when people are out this long that their bodies often begin to start shutting down, organ by organ.

'But David's organs haven't shut down,' Karen argued.

'Yes, that is true,' Dr. Mumford replied, 'but the longer this goes on the more his body will weaken. We need to be prepared for the worst outcome.'

Everyone knew the outcome they were talking about, but no one dared mention its name.

'What more can be done?' Ivan asked.

'We can't keep him on the ventilator indefinitely without seeing some signs of improvement. We have to be realistic and come to a decision that's best for David.'

'My David is not going to die,' Karen cried out. 'I will not accept this. And you, standing up and pointing her finger across the table at Dr Mumford, will not take him off that ventilator until I say so. He just needs time to recover.' Karen took a deep breath and sat down in her chair.

Dr. Mumford started to speak again, Mrs. Bonner we all realize what an emotional time this is for you and your family. We are trying to keep the communication open here and let you know the facts of the situation. You are obviously a religious woman so please prepare yourself and show David some mercy.

That was the last straw for Karen. She could hardly breath and inside knew she could not be a part of this conversation any longer and she got up and walked out.

Ivan who had come with her for support sat there not knowing if he should stay and hear if there was anything else to be said or get up and follow her. When Karen reached the door of the small conference room, she turned to him.

'Ivan, are you coming?'

He looked at her and knew that this was his cue to leave.

'Why don't you listen to the doctors?' Ivan said to her, once they were outside the conference room. 'They are the authority here.'

Karen whirled around on her heel.

'Don't you ever, say they are the authority,' she said in a slow, low, stern, no-nonsense voice. 'The only authority here is the Chief Physician, and that is our Lord Jesus Christ. If you are siding with them,' she motioned towards the elevator doors, 'then you need to go.'

Ivan stepped in front of her and started to reply when

Karen let out a low almost growling sound and pointed to the elevator.

'Call me if you need me,' was all he could manage to say as he walked away.

As she watched the elevator doors close, Karen began to cry. Never in her life had she felt so alone. Her only crutch to get her through this was her faith from on high.

Entering David's room, her heart was breaking, and she did not know what to do. When she saw Denise sitting beside her brother and reading to him, Karen brushed away her tears and walked over to them.

'I'm sure David is loving you reading his favorite book to him.'

'How do you know David can hear us?' Denise asked. 'How do you know David is going to wake up?'

'The same way you know?'

'But I don't know', Denise replied.

'Yes, you do. You are David's twin and you two have always had that special connection.'

'But Mom, I don't think I can feel it anymore.'

'Sure, you can. You are scared so you are blocking the feeling. What if the Doctor walked in here and told us that David should wake up tomorrow, would you be happy? Would you be able to feel him then?'

'Yes, I think so.'

'Well, I'm coming from the meeting and we were just talking about when David will wake up. We don't know when it will happen but trust me it will happen.'

'Are you sure Mom?'

'Yes, I'm sure. Now go back to reading for David,' Karen said, as she began praying to God from the depths of her heart:

'Lord, I am standing on Your promise to me and on the scripture that by Your stripes we are healed. So, I know David is already healed in Your precious name. Please send Your Angels of healing to help keep watch over him and to help him heal and wake up. Let Denise have her twin feeling again so that she will stand strong with me for David. I thank You for all these things in Your mighty name. Amen.'

As Karen sat there listening to Denise reading, she began gathering her thoughts on what had just happened in the meeting. Karen saw Ivan heading towards David's room and immediately got up and went out to meet him in the hallway. She was not prepared to let him into David's room. As Ivan approached, he put both hands up in a surrender gesture. When Ivan was close enough to her, he asked Karen to go down to the waiting room with him. They walked together down the hallway neither of them speaking. Ivan walked in first and gestured for Karen to sit down.

'I'm not changing my mind so save your breath if you're trying to change it.'

In a quiet voice, Ivan replied. 'I'm not trying to change your mind. I'm not here to fight. I just want you to talk to me and explain a couple of things.' His hand went up to signal to her that he was not done speaking. He sat down in the seat next to her and turned towards her. 'Karen do you know how much I love you and David and Denise? I don't want him to die. I want to turn the clock back and have pirate diners and play video games with the kids. And Karen I don't want you hurt. You and Momma have always told me that wisdom is the principle thing. So, I don't understand why you aren't listening to the wisdom that was in that room?' He kept his voice low and non-confrontational. He continued. 'Just tell me what you know that I don't know so I can believe as strongly as you do.'

Karen took his hand and squeezed it. 'Ivan do you not think that I am scared to death each day when I come here by what I might find. My worst fear looked me in the face that first day when I came back from picking up Denise from school. To see David on that ventilator felt like a knife stabbing into my heart and it has been slowly cutting through me each day. At night it is so hard for me as I don't want to leave him, but I know I must take care of Denise as well. I sometimes cry myself to sleep during my prayers.'

As her voice started to crack, and tears began to flow down her cheeks, Ivan pulled her close in a hug and Karen began to sob.

'Just let it out, sis. Let it out,' he whispered into her ear.

As Karen's sobs slowed Ivan reached over to the side table and grabbed the tissue box and handed it to her. She took a few tissues, blew her nose and wiped away the tears from her eyes. She took some more and blotted at his shoulder and started to apologize.

'Don't even apologize,' he said. 'What are little brothers for if not to cry on their shoulders?'

He smiled at Karen.

'Well, do you wanna know what I know?'

'Yes.'

'Do you remember the two things that Momma always said to us as we grew up? The first wisdom is the principle thing you remembered. But you forgot the second one.'

Ivan looked puzzled.

'We walk by faith not by sight. God has not told me to prepare for David's death. A long time ago He promised me I would have children and they would grow up and be used for his glory. God is not a man that He should lie. I am standing on his word to me. I cannot believe the doctors. They may have wisdom, but it is the practice of medicine. They don't really know when anyone will die. Only God knows. I need to get back down the hall and check on the kids.'

'Do you want me to come with you?'

'No, go home and get some rest. I'm going to sit and listen to Denise read to David for a while and then we'll head home.'

Tonight, she would listen to Denise read awhile as she did not have the strength to talk or drive right now. She just needed to recharge a bit before they headed home to get a good night's rest.

The drive home was quiet. A little over halfway home, Denise started to squeal with delight.

'What's the matter?'

'Nothing Mom, I can feel David.'

Karen glanced over at Denise and saw the biggest smile she had seen on her in weeks. That's when she knew she was right. David was going to come through this.

Chapter 12

A NEW DAY IS DAWNING

'But He was wounded for our transgressions,
He was bruised for our iniquities: The chastisement
for our peace was upon Him; and by his stripes
we are healed'

Isaiah 53:5

The morning seemed to come quickly. Karen reminded Denise that her grandmother would be picking her up at school and bring her to the hospital as she scooted Denise out the door to catch the school bus. Karen finished putting some more books in her backpack, looked around the room and headed out to the hospital. This was their 'new' morning routine.

When Karen got to the hospital she went straight to David's room. The nurses must have already been in to check on him. She sat next to his bed and held onto his hand. All she could was the sound of the monitors and of the machines doing their work. Her hope from last night was fading and doubts came to her that her son could die. The thought started a stream of tears to flow down her cheeks. Lost in her own thoughts she did not hear a nurse enter the room.

He walked quietly over to the opposite side of the bed where Karen sat holding David's hand. She had a bit of a start as she realized there was someone else in the room with them. Through the tears she saw a male nurse. This was new. She wiped at her eyes and picked up her purse fumbling to find a tissue.

'Can I help you?' Karen asked.

'You must be the mother that has everyone on this floor in a buzz. I came down to see for myself this formidable woman.'

'I don't know about formidable but yes, I'm David's mother,' Karen spoke, not sure what to think about this nurse.

'And, from what I've heard you are a very caring one,' the male nurse replied, as he turned around to face Karen offering her a handkerchief.

As she accepted the handkerchief she looked up and saw the kind brown eyes of this young man staring back at her.

'Karen why are you crying?

When Karen finished wiping away her tears.

'Why do doubts arise in your heart?'

Karen looked past him and stared lovingly at David lying there in the bed.

When the nurse spoke again her gaze returned to him.

'Are you seeking the dead here, you can see David is alive. Karen heard his words but puzzled at them.

He then bent down in front of Karen, so they were eye to eye.

Karen noticed the bold letters below his picture on his badge read Charge Nurse. She made eye contact again as he clasped her hands and looked deep down into her soul. She felt her heart began to burn with warmth and peace flooded into her. It was a warm soothing balm to her soul. Her eyes closed and in the soft tenor timber of his voice he said. 'You know, Faith From a mother's soul moves mountains.'

All the worries and doubts immediately left Karen and her head tilted back resting against the chair. With her eyes closed she let this warmth and peace penetrate deep within her soul and she knew without a doubt that today David would awake. He would live.

As the nurse left the room all Karen sat and watched him in complete silence. Moments later one of the regular nurses came into the room and she went over and started taking David's vitals.

'Didn't the other nurse do that when he was here?'

'What other nurse?' she replied. 'There's nothing on his chart.'

'But the charge nurse was just here.'

'Hmmm, that's kind of impossible as he's on his honeymoon.'

'Then who was just in here? Literally he just left?'

'I didn't see anyone in the hallway. What did he look like?'

Karen tried to describe, but she couldn't really remember what he looked like.

'There are only three nurses on the floor during a shift.' she replied as she finished taking David's vitals. 'If you remember what he looks like I'll be down at the nurses' station.'

This was crazy, why was Karen second guessing herself. She just finished a conversation with the charge nurse. For the time being Karen put it out of her mind. She had more important things to deal with.

Karen got up and walked out into the hall as soon as she saw her pastor friends get off the elevator. They hugged Karen and asked if there was any change in David.

'If you're asking if he's woken up yet, the answer is no,' Karen replied. 'But he is resting well and getting better every day. His body's gone through a lot and he needs lots of rest.'

Both looked at her with pity in their eyes.

'What are you giving me that look for?' said Karen.

'Karen, Ivan called us and told us about the meeting. Honey, we know you want to believe that David will be alright but with every day he doesn't wake up on his own he gets worse. We just want you to prepare yourself.'

'Pastor, I have it from the highest authority that my David is going to be just fine,' Karen said, feeling the need to set the pastor straight. 'He just needs extra rest to heal, but he is going to wake up and be just fine. So, if you are here to try and say anything differently to me, then I think you need to save your breath as I will not consider another alternative.'

There was almost a stare down between them.

Karen could see that she had hurt them with her words and inside she was asking the Lord for the right words and God seemed to take over.

'I know you mean well. But do you remember the daughter of Jairus. When Jesus told them, she was not dead just sleeping?'

'Yes', they replied starting to see where she was going.

'Well that is what is happening with David. He is sleeping.'

'It's not the same they started—'

Karen raised her hand to silence them and interrupted. 'I don't mean any disrespect, but David is going to wake up. If you do not believe in the power of Jesus, I ask that you go ahead and leave. I will take no offence as I know the doctors do not believe what I am saying. But I know God is our Jehovah Rapha and he always shows up on time.

Karen turned and walked back to David's room, leaving her pastors standing in the hallway with their mouths hanging open. They watched Karen and then turned and left.

When Karen entered David's room. She went over and turned on some of his favorite praise music, held his hand and prayed: '*God thank You for being my voice.*'

She heard Him, say: '*Stay strong in your faith and walk in the Word and the promise I gave you.*'

111

It was late afternoon when the doctors made their rounds. They were all there and Karen could see it was time. She saw Ivan through the doorway just getting off the elevator. She asked if they would mind waiting a moment until he got to the room. Whatever they had to say to her she wanted Ivan with her to hear them. Ivan walked in and went and stood next to Karen.

'Perfect timing brother,' Karen said. 'The doctors have just arrived, and I assume they have some news for me as they are all here.'

Dr Mumford started to tell Karen and Ivan that they thought it was best to go ahead and take the ventilator off David.

'Yes, it's time for him to breathe on his own,' Karen replied.

The doctors were a bit surprised at her quick agreement and went on to correct her.

'It is really unlikely that he will breath on his own for very long.'

'No, David will be able to breathe on his own,' Karen reassured. 'He is going to wake up and be fine. You'll see.'

With nothing more to say, the doctors moved to the other side of David's bed and began removing the ventilator and put a shot of something into his IV to help bring him around. The ventilator was off, and there was complete quiet in the room. David's eyes started to flutter.

'David, it is okay to wake up. Momma is here. I love you baby.'

Throughout, Karen kept her eyes closed as tears starting to roll down her cheeks when she felt them being wiped away and a tenor timbered voice in her ear said: '*open your eyes, look at David.*'

She did and saw the most beautiful brown eyes of her son looking back at her.

There was a weak cough followed by and even weaker voice saying,

'Mom, I'm thirsty,' David's spoke gently.

As tears rolled down her cheeks, Karen looked over at the doctors who stood there baffled.

'Drinking may be hard at first,' Dr. Rogers stepped up and said. 'Let's start with swabbing your mouth and then maybe some ice chips.'

He then started to check David's vitals and they were all normal. He listened to his lungs and they were clear. Dr Mumford came over and listened as well.

'We'll need to keep you a few more days,' Dr. Rogers said, 'to make sure you're strong enough to go home.'

'I just got here yesterday,' David replied, looking at him quizzically.

'Just rest right now David,' was all Dr. Rogers could say in reply.

Karen's prayers were answered. It was a miracle for sure and no one could tell her differently.

It took time to get David physically strengthened and back to where he was. He had to take summer school and work hard to catch up with his schoolwork. When he went back to school that fall David did not look the same. He had been transformed and made a new, like a butterfly that had emerged from a cocoon. The boyish looks turned into a handsome young man. He had no shortage of friends and they could not believe David had been so sick. There was still extra tutoring to be done that next year to get David totally caught up. Thank goodness he had a wonderful teacher, Mrs. Kohr who took an interest in him, going to bat for him with the school board so he could graduate with his class and not just put him back a year in school.

There were still struggles that they went through with David but in her heart, Karen knew the worst was over and the best was yet to come.

Finally, Graduation Day arrived, and Karen was feeling so proud to watch both Denise and David walk across the stage to get their diplomas. Another milestone in their young lives. Karen's tears of joy flowed and inside she was praising the Lord:

> *'Thank You, Lord, for letting us share this moment. I can hardly wait to see what else is in store for us for I know with You we can handle anything.'*

EPILOGUE

Ten years later...

Karen still lives in the house in Plymouth. She is active in her church and is considered a prayer warrior by many. She still works for the financial institution.

Karen's mom went on to be with the Lord five years after David was well.

Ivan drops by to help Karen with her honey-do lists when she has them. Ivan has changed jobs a few times, but he has become the rock that his family comes to when they are in need. He has not married but is in a relationship with a nice young woman.

After high school, Denise went on to the University and after graduation pursued a career as an accountant. She and David are still close. The twin bond will always be with them.

David works in sales job with a major department store and is doing well. He knows that God performed a miracle in his life and He and God are still working out all the details of where he can best use his talents.

'Bless the lord, O my soul; And all that is within me, bless His holy name! Bless the Lord, O my soul, and forget not all His benefits: Who forgives all your iniquities; Who heals all your diseases, who redeems your life from destruction and crowns you with lovingkindness and tender mercies.' Psalm 103:1-4

MEET THE INSPIRATION

Renee Emory Williams, first daughter of Lewis and Nellie Mae Emory, I have two siblings, Letisha and Andre, and two children. I've worked for a financial institution in the Midwest over 35 years.

I confessed the Lord when I was in my teens. I believe in the power of God and the Holy Spirit. My Godfather and Godmother, Rev. Willie O. Green and Evangelist Earlene M. Green were instrumental in furthering my spiritual beginnings. I was raised and lived with my Grandparents, Willie Whisby and Nellie Kate Whisby along with my mom and siblings. Grandma was a preacher's kid. Grandma always said to me everything is going to be alright. And she would often sing her church songs. We didn't have everything, but we had love and a sense of security.

MEET THE AUTHOR

Mary Albert grew up on a small farm in central Illinois with a curiosity for the world. Exploring the world through youth exchanges and then finishing her studies in Switzerland, Mary found the more she saw of the world the more she wanted to see. She chose the travel and hospitality industry as a way to feed her hunger for travel. In the process of traveling she saw many of the great and wonderful things that God put in this world. He gave every place in the world something special, one just has to open their eyes and their heart to see it.

God also gave Mary the gift of writing, so she can tell the stories not only of the places He made but also of the miracles that He performs in our daily lives. Mary befriended Renee at an ICCM conference and as their friendship grew, Renee started helping Mary with her faith journey by sharing her own. This became the inspiration behind *Faith From: A Mother's Soul Moves Mountains.*